LET'S GET MARRIED & DO EVERYTHING EXCEPT MAKE IT LAST

A heart-to-heart with men on loving and leading

ADRIAN N. CARTER

13TH & JOAN

13TH & JOAN

Published by 13th & Joan

13th & Joan
500 N. Michigan Avenue, Suite #600
Chicago, IL 60611
WWW.13THANDJOAN.COM

Ordering Information:
13th & Joan books may be purchased for educational, business or sales promotional use. For information, please email the Sales Department at sales@13thandjoan.com.

Printed in the United States of America

WWW.ADRIANCARTER.SOLUTIONS
WWW.EMPOWERMENCONFERENCE.COM

To men in need of a voice,
our society in need of growth,
and our hearts in need of healing.

"The unexamined life is not worth living."
– Socrates

THE WHY

INTRODUCTION

Writing this book was not easy. I avoided sitting behind the computer on many occasions to type and disclose my life for others to see my mistakes and shortcomings. It was never comfortable to do—but it was necessary. I've lived in the shadows for most of my life, suffering at the hands of abusive relationships. I've been secretive and have often allowed myself to be victimized. At the same time, I've made poor decisions, let my ego get the best of me, and hurt people in the process of dealing with my fears and hurts. Life eventually catches up to you, knocks you off your horse, and demands your attention and humility—and to add icing to the cake, life now demands that I share my story for the betterment of others, specifically men. In writing this book I'm reminded of the Apostle Paul's words in I Corinthians 15:9-11, "For I am the least of the apostles, that am not meet to be called an apostle, because I persecuted the church of God. But by the grace of God I am what I am: and his grace which was bestowed upon me was not in vain; but I labored more abundantly than they all: yet not I, but the grace of God which was with me. Therefore, whether it were I or they, so we preach, and so ye believed."

In spite of my shortcomings I know who I am in God. My pastor and mentor once said I have a zeal for God. I found that interesting because the story of King David deeply resonates with me. The Bible says King David was a man after God's own heart. Yet, we know the story of David to be a tempestuous one. I have had a tempestuous life. But I have come to find purpose in all of it. Every mistake and misfortune have slowly but surely cultivated me and the way I see the world. I see hurt people who hide behind smiles and laurels. I see a world of generational, cyclical abuse. I see abusers hidden in the shadows; they rain emotional terror onto their victims long after the act has ended. I see a world that highlights nonsense and undermines the valuable intangibles of life. The most audacious hurt I have witnessed and experienced is the breakdown of the family structure and marriage. That pain penetrated so deeply that I used to be able to feel the cells in my body cringe with fear and hopelessness.

Nonetheless, I am a man after God's own heart. And throughout these processes I've learned to become unapologetic about who I am, whose I am, and what I stand for. In so knowing, my goal is to walk in my purpose. My purpose is to develop leaders and visionaries, be a thought leader in building inclusion by challenging the way people think about normative views of our world, and raise awareness about the challenges and abuses men experience. I'm also a major advocate of love and successful intra and interpersonal relationships. I want to see men and women successful in marriages. Quite obviously, something is missing in our socialization process that has and continues to cause major breakdowns in marriages and families. The book was written to help men rethink their approach to relationship building, marriage, leadership, love, and conflict resolution.

Marriage is intended to be a blessing and an institution of great reward. But there is an ugliness that can come between two people, which when left unchecked can make marriage the most disastrous endeavor of one's life. Part of the ugliness is the social burdens and unbalanced expectations placed on men for ensuring marital success. Moreover, much of our Western society and other social mechanics around the world has domesticated, emasculated and subjugated men in ways that work against the success of marriage. In my goal to create leaders and visionaries, be an inclusive community-building thought leader, and create awareness on issues affecting men, this book uses my personal failures and successes to mentor men on the importance of knowing their worth, leading a purpose-driven life, knowing their lawful rights, understanding how to properly compartmentalize expectations, and challenging their thought processes on traditional values that have historically and unfairly boxed men in. This book is also intended to restructure the minds and hearts of men in how they view themselves and their spouse on a variety of topics that are gravely important to every marriage. The topics throughout this book offer a real-world, ontological point of view to show how bad the marriage can be if changes in the mind and heart are not made regarding the management, implementation, and expectations of marriage.

This journey began as I went through my separation and divorce. During that time, I began noticing certain patterns of communication from numerous men around me. Their communication about their role, failures, and the expectations of a man were startling, to say the least. As a result, I started talking and interviewing men throughout the community about their experiences in love, relationships, and marriage. Granted, I began to experience the car effect, where the make and model of the car you drive becomes overwhelmingly noticeable in comparison to other cars. The same car has always been on the road, but suddenly, now that you drive that car, you begin to notice an overabundance of that make and model. Similarly, I began to come across men who had story after story of relationships that failed and left them depleted in ways they felt were lopsided social norms that overlooked their efforts as men. I spoke to more than 50 men over the course of three years in the process of writing this book.

Many of these conversations came through social media, in person, at community events, and from men who reached out to me after hearing me speak on panels or post on social media. Many of them shared how they had no one to confide in because marital failure was seen as somehow their fault, more so than their wives'. They were willing to accept that they both contributed to its failure, but they too found a social world that projected misnomers of norms that upheld a very biased system toward men—men who were interested in doing right toward their spouse. It's a side of the story that's rarely told.

This book is also written with certain biblical precepts in mind and at times uses the King James Version of the Bible to underscore certain points. As a Son of God, I can only impart to you within the context of being a spiritual person who acknowledges God as the head of my life and has been saved through the sacrificial love of my Lord and Savior Jesus Christ. Overall, this book is a form of technological innovation in the heart as it relates to marriage and your relationship with self. This is all toward the end of empowering you to become a greater leader for your family, community, and finding success in your journey as a purpose-driven man.

LET'S GET MARRIED & DO EVERYTHING EXCEPT MAKE IT LAST

CHAPTER 1

Dear Adrian,

You have hit rock bottom. Many have before you and many more will after you. The fall is not the storyline. The comeback is: the getting up from the ground, the brushing off your knees, the stumbling, wobbly leg determination to stand, skid marks across the palm of your hands from trying to catch your fall. Banged up chest from the impact. Your shoulders may hurt. Your feelings may be sore. But it's about the comeback. It's the get up from disgrace. It's the rebuilding. It's the rebirth, the purification, the renewing of your heart and spirit. Even if you were set up, plotted against, now what? So what? They took their shot, it hit you in the chest, and you were bleeding out, consciousness fading. But here you are, still alive, breathing, wiser, smarter than you were before, and more watchful. You're better for this. You're a better human being. It's a story to tell. But more than just a story, it's a lesson to teach.

You have two young boys who will need this wisdom, your leadership and point of view to help through this circle of life. You will see this demon again and this time around know how to exorcise it. You did not do right—you did a lot of wrong. You did things unjustly and unfairly. You were not loving. You're complicit. Being confused, angry, hurt, brokenhearted, alone, and misunderstood was never a reason to do wrong. You know that now, better than some. You understand the consequences that come with wrong—and you're better for having learned it.

Love your kids. Do it for them. They need a happy, healthy, forgiving, and loving father. They will need a lighthouse and a beacon on their journey through these rough seas. And you will always know better than they how rough, deep, and dangerous these waters are. Count it a blessing that you went through it for them that one day your light, gained from these experiences, will be the very thing they need to get through their time of trials. Their trials will come. It will never be the case on this earth that trials do not come.

You have a daughter who will need you more than any other woman on this planet. You will be the love of her life for eternity on this earth. She's your obligation. Change the past by being her future. Change the past by making the future so bright that it burns through every misdeed from your past. You can do it. You have already done it. You have already walked this path in the future. You have to just be the real you, the future you, now in the present. Be your present self always, by being the future you, having learned from your past self.

Let go of the past. Let it go. God is still God. He will always be God. Don't fight him. It's a fight you can never win. Trust God. He knows you best. He knows your need. He even knew what you needed in this chapter of your life. He made you better. He made you real. He made you love. So love. Be love. Love Love and let Love love you back. God is Love. God loves you. He knows it hurts. What if God had no choice in the matter? I know you think God is God and always has a choice, but remember God plays by the rules. So you be fair to God. The Enemy may have petitioned God for your soul. And where wrongdoing was found was also found the evidence to touch your way of life. All of your doing was not always right. God knows the situation more inside out than you. So let him help you. You're not His slave. You're not here to be unwillingly brought into subjection like an animal. You're here to develop a relationship of trust and oneness. Your life is a worship; it's not the bowing down and learned ways of conducting business with God.

He wants your companionship and friendship and trust and conversation. God is a social God who loves to interact. God is a social spirit who wants to meme blessings into your life. He's holy, righteous, deals and plays in righteousness. And He's fun and loving, and caring, and loves a successful person who allows their success to come through Him and in His ways. God wants you to return home to Him so He can bathe you and shower you with blessings. He really wants to do that. He wants to sup with you and enjoy your company. He gets no pleasure in not having His son at home. Who in their right mind doesn't want their child home, in arm's reach, available, accessible, and vulnerable to their leadership and way of seeing the world? Give Him a chance, Adrian. Give Him another chance. He wants to bless you and give back to you what you've lost and more than you have ever considered gaining. But you have to go back to Him first. Rules are rules and He plays by the rules. Let Him love you again. Not that He has ever stopped loving you—but let Him love you again. And this time around you'll be more appreciative of it than ever before. From me to you. With love, Adrian N. Carter

I wrote this letter to myself while sitting at my desk at work, faced with the darkest hour of my life up to that point. I was going through a heartbreaking divorce after nine years of marriage to a woman I deeply loved and cared about. At the same time, my career could not get back on track in a field in which I once thrived. While facing these challenges, I found myself feeling failed by the church I grew up in since age seven, which in many ways rocked my spiritual foundation and left me feeling like another separation was simultaneously taking place with my divorce from my wife at the time.

It's been said before, and I agree, that divorce is worse than physically dying. In divorce, you watch death happen right before your eyes as you are forced to live through it as an eyewitness to your own demise, and quickly learn that you cannot testify on your own behalf. You are a co-conspirator to your own death, victim and victimizer, and it's all a very dark reality. The emotional toll was almost unbearable. After nearly nine years of marriage I found myself with a restraining order against me, forced out of my own home, sharing a lot less time with my children, and starting a new job that had not paid me yet. I was broken. I was terrified. I was in shock. It's as if a 26-year-old man and a 22-year-old woman had gotten together and said, "Let's get married and do everything except make it last."

Immediately after getting married I discovered a verbally abusive spouse who held no punches in minimizing my worth. The words that spewed from her mouth carried body bags. She later explained to me that she was overwhelmed with everything that had recently happened in her life. In less than three months of us being engaged, she had studied and passed her board exams, started her new job, married, purchased a home, and moved from her parents' home into our new condo. To add more to it, she also found my church of more than twenty years very unwelcoming. Most significantly, her job was intense. The 12-hour shifts took a serious toll on her body and spirit. I totally understood the weight she felt and tried to accommodate her.

The problem was that I was the place where all of her anger was taken out. My best attempts to make life easier were met with what looked like little to no appreciation, no reciprocity for my emotional needs, little to nearly no sexual relationship, and constant arguments. I bounced between not wanting to be in the marriage anymore, dedicated to being in the marriage because I had firmly believed God gave her to me as my wife, and simply not knowing what to do. I thought I was in the twilight zone. Things quickly spiraled out of control. I became verbally abusive back to her and we were both physically abusive to each other. While going through the divorce process, she revealed she had clocked out of the marriage after the first five months. Let's do the math on that: legally married for nearly nine years but emotionally divorced for eight and a half. How could anything good come from that?

I came into the marriage with a sincere dedication to being an upstanding husband. I had spent the past couple years prior to marriage focused on addressing areas I needed to grow in. I took the institution of marriage seriously and studied the topic. I had also observed some ways in my thinking and behaviors that had skewed my thoughts about women and relationships. For instance, I changed the music I was listening to. I observed that much of the lyrics in rap music were degrading of women and as a result, I had adopted a mentality that did not esteem them properly. I gained the understanding that treating my wife the way my father treated my mother was not the approach for me. Albeit we get a lot of our relationship cues from our parents, I came to understand that they are two different women (my wife and my mother) with different sets of needs being met by two different men.

I also took a very prayerful approach in selecting a spouse. I was very determined to not choose on my own. Accordingly, I sought the counsel of my spiritual leaders by presenting to them the woman who would later become my wife.

Now engaged, you would not have found a happier man in the Milky Way Galaxy. I remember sitting in the chair at my parents' home, holding a cup as my mom poured me some juice. I said, "Pour me more," in a boisterous, kingly voice. The loveseat where I sat had become my throne. My mother, in complete awe, said, "Adrian, I have never seen you so happy." She was right. I had never been happier in my life up to that point. I was happy because I felt I had approached the process correctly. It's like teeing off at golf. The ball was on the tee at the right height. My grip on the club was textbook, my feet were shoulder width apart, and my knees slightly bent. My approach was the proper form. And boy was I happy to be on this golf course of what I hoped would be marital bliss. But if you have ever played golf, then you know what any given round of golf can bring.

I did not have it all together. I was young, challenged with a pornography addiction, and prideful in my intelligence. I overcompensated in my behavior because of my insecurities. Knowing I had been sexually molested at the age of nine by a family friend always left me in a place of feeling less than adequate. My way of balancing the scale was to always present myself as a highly intelligent, social person in hopes of being likeable.

In spite of those challenges, my college years were my greatest years of maturation. I had excelled academically and socially in college, which rolled over into my professional career. Against the odds, my supervisor at the time gave me an opportunity to serve as interim director of my department and later, after receipt of my master's degree, I became the full-time director. It gave me good reasons to feel good about myself. There I was at 25 years old, working and progressing as a young Black professional.

But after marriage my social identity became more conflicted as the core of how I saw myself was immediately challenged by my wife at the time. I was managing a half-million-dollar budget at work, but my wife immediately challenged my knowledge on money management. I was a leadership development trainer, coordinating and implementing leadership development programs at work, but at home my feedback had no weight in helping to resolve matters in our marriage or her job situations. In whatever category I saw myself as a competent person with something to offer, it became a glaring area of conflict. Aside from a paycheck and sperm for procreation, it appeared as if I brought little to the table. Certainly, I wasn't always wise in how I dealt with situations, but I came into the marriage with a zeal for my wife and a commitment to our relationship. I was serious about being a loving, affectionate provider, protector, and accountable husband. But I started to feel inadequate.

Having children was the glue to our marriage at the time. After a little over a year of marriage, she came out of the bathroom with a wide smile, said, "Happy Father's Day," and announced she was pregnant. It was amazing to see the glow from my wife at the time during the first two trimesters. She was the prettiest woman on the planet. But that did not change our communication style to one another or the tension that hovered over our household.

I looked forward to being a father. After our first child's birth, I explained that I wanted to learn everything about taking care of our child including how to feed him, change him, make his bottles, check the bottle temperature, clean him, hold him, put him to sleep, interact with him, and whatever else was necessary. I was a hands-on dad. We took turns feeding the baby every two hours as our newborn slept between us surrounded by a pillow brigade.

But that happy moment quickly changed. One night I forgot to bring something into the bedroom as part of prepping his bottles. She reminded me, and I responded saying I'd do it later. I was already in the bedroom and did not want to go back to the kitchen. She immediately fired back with some choice words. I was really taken aback. It came from left field. She dug in some more. I decided to go to the kitchen and get the forgotten item because, apparently, not getting the item seemed to have caused such a visceral response. As I walked past the foot of the bed I stopped and asked her, "Why are you talking to me like this? Everything has been so good between us. Where is this coming from? I'm the father of your child, doesn't that mean anything?"

Her response rocked my world to the core and sent me spiraling back into that twilight zone. She looked me square in the eye and replied, "I don't give a fuck who you are..." and her tsunami of words continued. Her words took the air out of me. I felt so discouraged. I walked out of the bedroom to the kitchen in a trance, stopped to adjust the thermostat and along the way clocked out of the marriage. I was numb. I thought having our first child would result in a positive shift in our marriage. It did not.

I clocked out and *decided to do wrong.* I said to myself that if she did not appreciate me doing right then I'd just do wrong—biggest mistake of my life. My untamed emotions spilled over into my job. Hurt from my marriage, I found myself involved with someone on my job who later used that relationship to accuse me of sexual harassment in an effort to save her job. That was another crushing blow to the marriage. My employers uncovered the truth and acknowledged that sexual harassment did not occur. But my contribution to the circumstance hurt me more than anyone else as it put my job and career on the line and painted an ugly stigma and reputation amongst my colleagues and counterparts.

The pattern of hurt-me-and-I'll-hurt-you-back was in full swing throughout the marriage. Some of it was ignorance, but all of it was a deep pain I constantly felt from trying to please the world around me: my wife, my church, my job, and myself. It always felt as if I was coming up short no matter how much I tried. By year eight of our marriage, I seriously considered suicide and wrestled with it more during the divorce process. I wrote the following poem, *100 Reasons to Live*, to help me through.

100 REASONS TO LIVE

a poem

I had to come up with one hundred reasons to not take my
life. Apart from the obvious, like my two sons and one
daughter (which most would think is more than enough),
I needed more reasons than them. So I wrote one hundred
reasons to live.
I concur that one reason is more than enough but when

you feel stuck in a relationship with no relations and only shipwrecking conversations, sometimes you want to give up. Not that this person is everything, but when the court gives them everything—your manhood, the kids, the house, your right now, and half of your pension—no matter how hard you tried or how hard you cried, when all your life savings wasn't monetary and they terminate you from the job you paid more attention to, you sometimes need more than one reason to live.

The very first reason that came to mind was Nehki. He's 14 years old and a budding musician and music engineer. I know he looks up to me although our conversations are few. Musically, I am what he wants to do. I am a simple chord progression to his Beethoven's 5th. He is a musical younger me with a greater gift. But if I took my own life, would I take a piece of his melody? Would my suicide leave a note sustained in him that augments his fingers to not see life brighter than middle C? The dissonance between the weight and using music as an escape might be a very slow and dreary song. So I live for his music to have life.

My fifty-second reason considered I might be a restaurant, ringing up the order for which I've been prepared for that one appointed customer. It's possible that my life story may contain ingredients sautèed through my experience to serve and be of service to this individual who hungers and thirsts for righteousness. Not that I've done all things right, but you can learn a lot from a dummy. I'll tell this appointed customer that life is more about the aftertaste than indulging in the first bite. So I live to be a nutrient to the life of that customer.

My ninety-ninth reason was simple: Maybe I've already died. And to take my own life would just be redundant, maybe that's why caterpillars cocoon. They hope to die and in the midst of it. Find one hundred reasons to butterfly.

Number eight: It's not fair for a father to bury his son.
Number thirty-seven: Is that the last thing you want to be remembered for?
Number forty-two: You can't change your mind after it's done.
Number twenty-five: The life insurance won't pay out in the first three years.
Number eleven: I think my mother would really be hurt.
(She was upset that I let Thanksgiving and Christmas pass without calling.)
It appears I have to get through life on this side before I find out
Suicide communications don't get through at all.

Number one hundred: Maybe it's not all of me that needs to die—just the part of me that wants to commit suicide. It's an elixir in my bloodstream. The antidote from the snakebite contains the same venom. So I might have just gotten half of this right as I'm trying to die out of this skin. Maybe I only need to shed this skin and live. I have a hunch that on the other side of this life we live is a bad science non-fiction movie that replays the worst day of your life to see if you can get 100 of those moments right.
I needed to be one hundred percent sure. No second-guessing about the seconds left to make this decision. Maybe Fallopian tubes are conference rooms where conception

has the same conversation about finding reasons to live. My father and mother found one reason to have me. It appears I'm doing what they may have done 'cause if you can find one reason to live, then you can find a hundred and one.

After a year into our marriage I vividly remember sitting on the edge of the couch, crying to her, asking, "Why don't you make love to me? Why don't you pay me any attention? *What's wrong with me*?" After all, I was being an upstanding citizen to her and fulfilling my husbandly duties as best I knew. But if I was doing everything I knew to be this excellent husband, and she's somehow not receptive to it, then what was the matter? I concluded ultimately something was wrong with me—clearly, I was the problem (as paradoxical and confusing as it may have been).

Receiving very little affection, attention, or appreciation from my spouse at the time subsequently clouded my judgment with anger, resentment, and issues of self-worth. I was emotionally broken down by my marriage within the first year. Remember, at the point of divorce was when she revealed that she had checked out of the marriage after the first five months. These emotions fueled me to continuously make bad decisions throughout the marriage. Within eight years we had both been domestically violent, verbally abusive, threatening, tit-for-tat, and unforgiving until it all came crashing down.

The biggest shocker was that people mistook us for having a good marriage. We were both young, college educated, career professionals, and had the appearance of a good physical match. But much of that was an attempt to keep up a good public image, a matter that further troubled me for years during the marriage. The marriage was abusive behind closed doors, yet she demanded a good public face. On the other hand, I was demanding help. I eventually came to a place where I stopped accepting that it was okay to be abused in private and act like everything was okay in public. By year eight I realized that I had been married to someone who had never taken the time to acknowledge, validate, uplift, or prioritize me as first in the relationship. I realized that from day one of the marriage I was in a constant mode of giving and rarely receiving.

In hindsight, the pattern was set from the wedding planning. We had first agreed to a wedding list of 100 guests. After she and her mother determined everyone they wanted to invite, the number grew to 136, with 100 of the guests being for her family. I was only left with 36 slots. I acquiesced for the sake of maintaining peace. However, the disparity was systemic throughout the marriage.

Fueled by my church teaching plus being an individual who found it easy to give to others, I found myself constantly giving in to her desires for the sake of peace. Using Scripture, my pastor instructed me that I needed to decrease so she could increase. But how much of myself do I depreciate so she can appreciate, when does it balance out, and where do you draw the line?

It did not all happen overnight. But I rarely felt the reciprocation of love. Many more things were said and done in the marriage. But what's most important is what I learned from them and what I believe is important for you as a man or young man to know so if and when the time comes, you can avoid the pitfalls and mistakes I made and get married and make it last.

THE MALE MARITAL DIASPORA

CHAPTER 2

While separated and going through the divorce process, I discovered an unforgiving world that minimized the realities, emotions, and experiences men encounter in relationships. I painfully learned the societal response to my divorce was that men aren't allowed to be emotional. Men aren't supposed to ask for alimony—that's a thing for women to do. Men aren't supposed to cry (for too long, if at all). Men are supposed to cut their losses and move on. Men are supposed to become adept at bearing the weight of the world on their shoulder. In fact, a good man is supposed to give the world to his woman while simultaneously carrying her and the world on his shoulders. Ultimately, men are supposed to accept accountability for the demise of the relationship, man up and move on—and that's pretty much where it starts and ends.

Between the conglomerate of family, acquaintances, and my church leadership, I was made to feel bad for feeling bad. I remember my father saying that I had lost the affection of my wife. Apart from not being convinced I'd ever had her affection, I understood what my father was saying. But I turned and asked him a question. "Why is it that she couldn't have lost my affection?"

He looked at me puzzled and walked away. What I was really asking him was, "Why am I not worth losing? Why is it always about her needs and desires, her approval or disapproval?" There appeared to be a general assumption, including from my church leadership, that my marriage's demise was mostly my fault. The man is supposed to be the head of the household and the covering for his wife, and somehow, I had failed at that. The Scriptural basis is that Adam and Eve were not removed from the Garden of Eden until after Adam ate the fruit. Eve's eating of the fruit was impactful but not the most consequential act. This is the (misguided) burden of patriarchy.

There were some acknowledgements by my church leaders regarding how difficult a woman my wife was at the time, but the expectation remained that a "real" man should know how to reach her in the state she was in. Therefore, failure was reflective of headship, ultimately the man's fault—ultimately, my fault. This drew a clear picture to me: the woman is almost always the victim, and the man is almost always the victimizer. I've since learned that that line of reasoning is unhealthy, dare I say ungodly, and destructive at its roots amidst a social climate meant to distort the role of a man.

The pattern of the lack of accountability amongst women and the mischaracterization of headship as the role of a man had become so obvious to me by then that I felt I had no worth. Society had deemed me a failure, as did my wife at the time. Essentially, I found very little support for what I was experiencing. I realized profoundly that I wasn't allowed to be a victim (albeit I was a battered husband who had experienced domestic violence, verbal abuse, and sexual abuse from a spouse who had been very manipulative and controlling). Realizing these truths at that moment caused suicidal thoughts and depression to weigh heavily on me.

THE MARITAL DIASPORA

The most revealing lessons about society and myself occurred during my time of separation as I experienced what I call the *male marital diaspora*. The term diaspora is typically associated with groups of people being displaced or dispersed from their original locations.

Men experience emotional displacement when they are forced into socially created roles that fall outside the individual's purpose for living. The overwhelming emphasis on a man to provide and protect makes it appear as if a man's categorical function is to simply generate an income to take care of his family and utilize his muscles to physically protect her. Categorical function means that that is his essential function in life. These socially created roles result from a socialization process that over-imposes social compliance onto men through religion and law, which subsequently distracts them from being purpose-driven men. Another term for this is gynocentrism. I came to understand my own diaspora as I began to examine the mechanisms of the burden of relationships, the impact of my fractured self-identity, the role of my ego, and the impact of some common messages found in my church.

BURDEN OF RELATIONSHIPS

There are many veiled or silent expectations that men must meet throughout their rites of passage to manhood. In many instances, it's expected of men to understand and know their role by default of being a man, in spite of a woman's shortcomings. A major part of a man's role includes uplifting the woman because women, allegedly, have a more demanding role in society. Her harder role is a mixture of her being the physically weaker sex, the emotional rollercoaster of their menstrual cycle, domestic duties while working full-time, maintaining her health and beauty, being sexually available to her husband, dealing with cattiness on the job, and the overall pressures of maintaining certain ideals of marriage.

But who supports the husband? If we were to place the woman's greater emotional needs and expectations into a box, and if the man, her significant other, is responsible for lifting that box, then who bears the bigger burden? The legs of men collapse under the weight of women who believe their man should uplift them and who also believe that men, by definition of being a man, do not need similar support. And women like this exist. Some are subtle and some are direct in exposing their school of thought, but a woman can be just as destructive in a marriage as a man because society allows her to hide under the guise of victim, even after she has victimized the man.

Statistically, men commit suicide 3.5 times more often than women and married men are twice as likely to commit suicide as opposed to married women.[1] Why are men killing themselves? One contributing factor is because we live in a society that weighs heavily on men with overbearing expectations; yet the social conversation (especially from women) is about how hard it is to be a

---

1 Source: https://afsp.org/about-suicide/suicide-statistics/

woman. It's rare to hear a man say it's hard being a man. He would most likely get laughed out the door.

But when it comes to the institution of marriage, it appears society is rigged against men in the space of marriage. Our society places higher levels of accountability for the marriage, fatherhood, and matters of divorce, and the corresponding stigmas, more heavily onto the man. Even in instances where the woman was an obstructionist to the marriage's success, she is still somehow the victim of the divorce.

In one of his most prolific sermons, Pastor T.D. Jakes preached that one of the most profound things he has come to understand is the emotional, spiritual, and psychological warfare was designed to place women in captivity and kill men. His words, found on YouTube under the heading "The Enemy Is After the Man☒," insightfully dissect the difference between men and women and shed tremendous light on the silent pain men endure that leads to higher suicide rates among them. ☒☒☒☒☒☒☒☒☒☒☒☒☒☒☒☒☒☒☒☒☒☒☒☒☒☒☒

In a nutshell, men are faced with challenges on a daily basis with mounting expectations that are equally or more overbearing than women, yet they find a world that says you should be able to handle it by the fact you are biologically a man. And that is not true. Men are not endowed with any greater gifts than women. ☒☒☒☒☒☒☒☒ ☒☒☒☒☒☒☒☒☒☒☒☒☒☒☒☒☒☒☒☒☒☒☒☒☒☒☒☒☒☒☒☒Men carry the burden of relationships and are met with far less emotional support in society—the same society that has not permitted men to emote. The message of manhood has domesticated men to being mostly viewed as over-sexual beings, financial providers, and protectors.

FRACTURED SELF-IDENTITY

I've struggled with issues of self-worth for the majority of my life. Sexual molestation at the age of nine left me with a severely fractured sense of self. I was introduced to pornography and bullied by an older kid who forced me into sexual acts that no children at any level should be exposed to. It was a dark cloud over my life throughout my middle and high school years. I never knew how to be comfortable being me, not when I knew I was "damaged goods." Notice the question I asked my wife at the time at the edge of the couch: "What's wrong with me?" I grew up most of my life feeling, almost certain, that something was wrong with me.

I had married the perfect person to uncover all of my flaws and fears, especially with a severely fractured identity due to sexual abuse. Like many marriages, we were confronted with matters regarding the in-laws and extended family members, saving money, church attendance, and decisions about raising children. But the insecurities I had were evident and the Enemy that comes to kill, steal, and destroy used my wife at the time to relentlessly attack me in very profound ways. (Note to self: are we putting this on the Enemy using her, which absolves her of being accountable for her actions? Was it a matter of her own insecurities that she needed to identify, accept, and deal with? Do I get to say the Enemy used me? Or am I simply held responsible as a man because I am the man? Am I making allowance for her, a victimizer, to not appear as a victimizer?)

On a handful of occasions when arguments flared up, my wife at the time would tell me to go back to the guy who sexually molested me. She also repeatedly told me something was sexually wrong with me and insisted I was hypersexual. I sought therapy at the age of 31 for the sexual molestation I had experienced as a child. It helped greatly. The therapist cleared up beliefs and misconceptions about being hypersexual, concluding my sexual behavior was normal for a healthy male my age. But even after therapy my wife at the time still insisted something was wrong with me. I felt indicted throughout much of the marriage. I felt sexually broken because sex was used as a weapon against me. At one point during the marriage, I made sure to not get naked in front of her. I would strip down to just my underwear, then step into the bathtub and finish undressing. Clearly, in my mind at the time, I was undesirable and felt something must have been wrong with the way I looked.

EGO

I had been broken for far too long. I needed to heal. I needed to take responsibility, accountability, and control of my life. Part of that included learning humility. My ego was at the center of it all: my ego to save myself, to be respected and loved, to gain the affection and attention from my spouse that I thought I was rightfully owed, and being heard when I had spoken. The actions of my wife during that phase of my life may have been emotionally and spiritually undermining. But my actions and reactions, things I had control of, made things profoundly worse for the marriage and for myself. I would have been better off dying for righteousness' sake than trying to defend myself against her. I was emotionally out of control and always trying to seek revenge. I was wrong and, in the process, contributed to my marital demise.

Understand the issue with ego was not in what my expectations were. My expectations were appropriate. The ego showed itself when the expectations were not met. The ego also showed itself when I retaliated to verbal abuse with verbal abuse. The ego showed itself when I retaliated to her sexual deprivation by pursuing the sexual affection of other women. The ego showed itself when I felt disrespected and took my anger out on the wall. While separated from my wife at the time, I learned my ego had to go. One of the most beautiful things happened to me during this time. In the space of learning to let my ego go, in humility, I began to find myself.

UNWORTHINESS & VALIDATION

I have found much of the messaging in religion to be bathed in unworthiness. A common premise of the church is that you are a sinner in need of God's grace and saving, and you would be unworthy of life if not for the mercy of God. Moreover, as a pastor's son my entire life, I grew up in a church where I was often the "example" of being sinful, along with a handful of other members in the church. I realized that the imposed need for validation from my church contributed to my sense of unworthiness. Imposed because the culture of my church leadership consistently and publicly reprimanded or praised me based on their perception of what was rightful behavior. I experienced a lot of internal confusion because my efforts to meet the standards of marriage, church, work, and self did not always make sense to me. In the process I experienced a lot of internal conflict and failed expectations.

In summary, between the poor perception of myself from being sexually molested, the unworthiness of self from the church message, an overall emotionally abusive marriage, and my ego fighting to have presence, it is no wonder I walked in a state of confusion and pain for so long. In fact, I often felt deserving of the abuse and manipulation within the marriage, because, after all, I was a sinner who had not gotten it right—at least that is what I believed at the time. Fortunately, during this season of separation with impending divorce, I began learning to accept responsibility for my contributing behavior, repent for my pride, and abase myself. I began to understand the importance of doing the right thing at all costs. And not just doing the right thing because it's right to do, but because doing the right thing was a part of my character. I also learned to stop being confused about who I am, what I am, and whose I am. I am a father, leader, author, poet, philanthropist, speaker, educator, comedian, defender of the North, guardian of the Southern Gates, a god, romancer, lover, art and artist, husband, songwriter, music producer, sound engineer, leadership development trainer, conflict resolution practitioner, thought leader, masseuse to the deserving, revolutionary without the fist, master chef of gourmet spaghetti, keeper of a clean house, and a difference maker. I learned that God, both creator of man and woman, desired the best for me, desired to see me prosper, reach great heights of success, and touch the lives of galaxies. I learned that the accountable thing to do is make myself a living example of my failures and success in love so others will know what a broken and contrite heart looks like and learn from my mistakes.

THE SOCIAL CONVERSATION & SOME GREAT MISNOMERS

CHAPTER 3

I stood in line at the grocery store at the checkout counter behind a much older woman. My groceries started to mix in with hers, at which point, I jokingly said that she could go ahead and pay for them. The older lady laughed. But the lady cashier interjected and said, "You're supposed to pay for them." Somewhat surprised, but not surprised, I replied, "No. She can too." And then it started.

"You're the man, you're supposed to pay," the cashier said.

"But what if she makes more money than me?" I asked.

"It doesn't matter; you're the man," she insisted.

"But she could be a multimillionaire and I work for pennies. Why wouldn't that matter?"

"Well, the man is supposed to pay."

"Obviously, the woman and I are not in a relationship, but it shouldn't be *just* because I'm the man I should have to pay," I continued when it was my turn for the cashier to ring up my groceries. "It's something we're supposed to do together."

"I know," she responded. "I have a boyfriend and he and I both pay toward things all the time."

"Why then are you telling me to do something different from what you practice?" I asked.

THE SOCIAL CONVERSATION

And that's the social conversation at work. The social conversation is the socio-normative rules we restate and reiterate throughout society. It is nomenclature that is upheld against our knowing better and doing differently. Anywhere you find people gathered for an extensive period of time (in the grocery store, salons and barbershops, or at the water cooler), you will find in-depth conversations reiterating norms and rules that subjectively reinforce beliefs about what we are supposed to be expecting, practicing, and tolerating in relationships.

Social media plays a pivotal role in this new era of the social conversation. Social media has become a platform for all perspectives to be shared, liked, debated, and relayed throughout society. Memes of every kind are circulated throughout the ether in support of some notion or the other in this ever-growing social conversation. Many of them are covertly expressed as humor. While humor is an undeniable medicine of the soul, a meme is never *just* a meme. A meme is an imprint in the social conversation that communicates and reinforces specific ideals. What makes a joke funny is its truth. Likewise, the truth of the meme still communicates an ideal.

Unfortunately, much of the social conversation is misleading because it is saturated with perspectives of people with varied experiences and varied outcomes in relationships that have been maintained in various contexts. The social conversation is centered on the ideal. However, an overwhelming amount of people do not live these ideals, which means that every variation of family is a new ideal that requires a new set of rules. For example, the ideal of a married heterosexual relationship is usurped by divorce, creating a new ideal for divorcees. Now as a divorcee seeking to enter another marriage, what is the ideal for a blended family? What is the ideal if the divorcee prefers a spouse with no children while already having their own children? What is the ideal waiting time before marrying again? What is the ideal time for introducing them to your children? What is the ideal marriage ceremony considering the first marriage had the big hoopla wedding with the white dress, yet it still ended in divorce?

You will find an answer for each question in the social conversation based on someone's first-hand or hearsay experience. The web of ideals is ever-growing as we live in a more connected world. Blanket solutions to these ideals are fruitless because they do not capture the nuance of individual culture, perspectives, or the deeper emotions motivating the individual. The only effective ideal is YOUR newly negotiated ideal.

SOME GREAT MISNOMERS

Men and women share a variety of experiences that are positive and negative, direct and indirect that have shaped their view of marriage and the opposite sex altogether. People in general have also shaped their ideas of marriage based on what they have observed from marriages around them, including their own parents, guardians, and extended family, in addition to religious teachings and what's projected through popular culture on television, radio, and the overall media. Unfortunately, popular culture usually seeks to exploit stereotypes or use satire as a form of entertainment. Those reinforced images tend to do more tainting of the truth about how relationships actually work than depict marital reality. Unfortunately, both men and women draw certain conclusions and expectations about love, marriage, and relationships that create barriers before either party has encountered each other.

I have come to recognize some of those looming conclusions and expectations that men encounter. Many of these expectations are projected on to us, and we have historically accepted them. But in order to come to a clearer sense of self, we first have to eliminate some of these popular but deepened ideas we have inherited from the world around us; they are presented as facts, when in fact, they are misleading concepts. Walking around with these beliefs places undue pressure on you. I call them the great misnomers. A misnomer is an inaccurate or misleading presumption.

#1 Practice vs. Values

People love to pronounce how they value tradition. Tradition is a warm, comfortable blanket that feels more familiar than factual. However, the economic shifts of our times have created new ideals that many people struggle to adopt. As such, the social conversation, spaces that allow people to share and exchange, is bombarded with value statements that are contrary to practice. Many of these values have been taught to people from their religious background, corroborated through their personal experience, passed down as tradition from family and friends, and reinforced through popular culture.

Many people live in social-emotional conflict zones in which they struggle to find balance in their stated values versus the reality of life. This happens when people attempt to hold on to traditional values amidst a changing world. For example, the traditionally upheld belief that the man/husband is the breadwinner is a failing notion in the 21ST century when considering the educational and economic advancement of women. The median household income for a married couple is close to $80,000/year, greater than a single person at approximately $55,000/year. A married couple with children will find it extremely difficult to survive on the salary of a working husband at that median salary. Inflation, the cost of living in major metropolitan areas, and the lack of salary increases has made it necessary for 62 percent of married couples with children to have a two household income.[2]

Let me paint you another scenario of how practice and values sometimes clash. Imagine a conservative Republican household that is pro-life with strict Christian values who find out their underage daughter is pregnant. The father, a politician, has an upcoming election. The driving forces in the decision-making process far outweigh any social commentary about how to handle the situation. With an impending campaign, the media reports may call into question the candidate's Christian and conservative values, which may impact voter turnout for re-election. What will the candidate do? Will practice meet or depart from their family values? We have plenty more examples of leaders, such as politicians and pastors, who profess one ideology but are later found to practice a lifestyle alternative to their professed value system. People do the

2 https://www.bls.gov/news.release/pdf/famee.pdf

same in relationships, such as the cashier mentioned at the beginning of this chapter.

#2 The Traditional Woman (Never Really Existed)

You will find many women and some men in the social conversation asserting their traditional values, mostly believing in the domestic/homemaker role of women and the financial/breadwinner role of men. The traditional woman tends to assert that it is optional for women to have gainful employment, but a mandate for men. She would often maintain this belief even when she is employed (note the break between practice and values). However, the practice of that belief system falls apart, largely because you cannot be selective about what traditional values to enforce from a certain time period while ignoring other factors.

If a woman or man claims to be traditional when it comes to relationships, then she or he must maintain the other traditions that come with the time period from which they are pulling these concepts. If you or she want traditional gender role values and practices from the 1950s, then you have to value and practice everything from the 1950s—there is no a la carte. You must also include the economic, political, religious, and social aspects of the time period. Markings of a traditional woman in the 1950s include the ability to cook and clean, sew and knit, and garden; less likely to drive a car; not see higher education as a premium; not be entrepreneurial; if working, work as a secretary or frontline employee only—not as the CEO or boss of men; be a virgin or practice abstinence if divorced; and live with your parents (especially your father) until marriage. A woman who says she is traditional needs to meet these qualifications at minimum. Otherwise, she is simply picking and choosing and reinforcing ideals that favor her and overlooking the entirety of the time period from which she is pulling these values and practices. It is important to note, the traditional construct of gender roles from the 1950s were created for only one type of ideal for one type of women: white middle-class women.

I question, why not pull a value system and practices from the 1850s, 1300s, or some time before Christ? The 1950s is preferred because it speaks to a timeframe that is most advantageous to women, a timeframe in which they were not required to have gainful employment. However, that is an extremely uninformed view because the expectations of white middle-class women in the 1950s were different for women of other classes and race.

In a lot of cases, what you find in the 21ST century are women who want access to upward mobility through higher education and career development, but not the responsibility that comes with it. In other words, she wants to be educated and increase her earning potential, but not have the same level of financial responsibility for the relationship. Somehow, this is the responsibility of the man, even when he is paid less than her. She claims that traditionalism exempts her from the financial responsibility of the marriage while allowing her the flexibility to take advantage of making money. However, in many instances that is more of a stated belief (a value statement) in the social conversation than it is a practice. Most relationships operate as a shared communal effort that pulls on the contributions of both parties regardless of their income.

Another question comes to mind: Why is the woman only suitable as a homemaker? What rationale underpins this approach? Historically, the woman has simply been viewed as incompetent in matters of leadership. It is a tactic of hegemony, power displayed by men to rule over women and other categories of people who are further demeaned and disqualified to live this idealized version of life. Women have been historically bundled into one package of weakness.

There is no such thing as a traditional woman. The notion of a traditional woman only speaks to an idealistic presentation of marriage that reflects a particular class and culture of people. It is a popularized concept built out of patriarchy, male hegemony, and beliefs that consider the woman as the emotionally, financially, and intellectually weaker human.

On the contrary, women have been shattering these illegitimate notions for eons. To discuss practices from a certain time period only provides a snapshot of a specific group of people in a particular political, economic, or social class. As such, practices of the 1950s cannot be sustained in the 21ST century amidst the numerous ideals that people encounter, changes in the law, the Women's Suffrage Movement, feminism, and overall support for equity of minority groups, including women. Women are not a monolithic group that needs to meet the standard of a dominating male class. Women, like hair, come in many different textures, colors, length, and depth of roots. And like hair, some are in great condition and others are in need of varying levels of care. However, women are equally complicit in propping up these male hegemonic notions because they have found a way to benefit from these social constructs as well.

#3 The Expectation of Knowing

The expectation of being a man is a very tall order. While what it means to be a man is defined on a sliding scale reflective of an individual's direct and indirect experiences, culture, and spiritual beliefs, there is a common thread that I found runs through most feedback whenever I ask the question what does it mean to be a man: it is expected for a man to know. To know what? Not everything, but almost everything; specifically, how to lead and all of its encompassing components: how to pray, manage, effectively communicate, strategize, father, pick up the pieces, repair things around the house, have world knowledge, be well-exposed and well-versed, move in and out of various circles, and whatever else comes to mind. And if you need to learn these things, then learn quickly.

On the other hand, a woman's expectation to know is usually centered on domestic duties such as cleaning, cooking, and washing. In many instances, women are expected to manage the finances brought in by the man. Women also face major expectations regarding their image. However, the expectation of a woman is usually not to **lead and strategize** for the overall vision of the marriage. Noting the difference in expectations between the genders translates into the following:

- The social expectation of being a man is ultimately greater than the expectation of a woman because
- The greater expectation places a greater level of responsibility and accountability for the success of the marital relationship onto the man, and thereby,
- The failure of the relationship is placed more heavily onto the man.

And when men buy in to these expectations, turn around and not live up to them, they easily fall prey to being shunned by the same men and women who helped to define the social norm of what it means to be a man. It is an overwhelming and unforgiving expectation to live up to. Couple that with the social expectation that men should be better at managing their emotions because being emotionally expressive (crying, moody, attitudinal, etc.) are considered dispositions reserved only for women. These men are often labeled as effeminized, an emasculating tactic promulgated by both men and women.

So what are you left with as a man: a high expectation to know (and to not show signs of weakness in your emotions). You would think men are robots. And in many ways, they are. I understand that women share these sentiments when they are sexually objectified. Similarly, men are also sexually objectified and further objectified as tools of protection and provision. Men buckle under this unreal and overbearing expectation to both know with very little opportunity to be emotionally-centered.

Knowing how to navigate life in its varied forms is not automatic. Men, as a husband, you will do most of your learning in the marriage; you learn how to be a husband while married and she learns how to be a wife while married. And neither of you will be much wiser than that prior to marriage. Subsequently, you must allow yourself this freedom to learn as you go. As a matter of fact, in most instances how would you know to manage a relationship with one specific woman on a day-to-day basis by catering to her spiritual, emotional, and physical needs, maintaining the cars, fixing things around your home, managing the bills and expenses, managing the childbearing process, making parenting decisions regarding discipline, education, and extracurricular activities, building a vision for the family legacy, fixing meals, maintaining a clean environment, managing yourself and the responsibilities on your job, establishing family time, being involved with a church, mentoring group, or professional organization, ALL WHILE effectively communicating, resolving conflict, problem-solving, and maintaining your own spiritual, emotional, and physical needs? I'll wait.

On the flip side, a wife wants to be included and acknowledged for her knowledge base. She may feel that her educational level and experiences can appropriately influence the discussion or decision-making process of her husband. The disconnect comes in the expectation of the man's leadership capacity to finalize the decision in his "know best" role, even when she feels that she knows best on a particular matter. Upon closer inspection, you will observe that this is not so much an issue of knowing, but an issue of accountability. He ultimately has to know more because he is ultimately more accountable for successful outcomes in the marriage. A string of poor decisions or poor judgment leads to a lack of trust and possibly revolt against his leadership. So even when she knows more, he still has to know more, even if that means knowing when to utilize her knowledge base over his.

Men, I implore you to rid yourselves of this misnomer. You do not need to know everything in order to be in a successful marriage. You are a human being, just like a woman is, who has experienced ups and downs, sunny and rainy days, moments of loneliness and of sharing, maybe abuse of one kind or another, and passages of healing. You have and are experiencing life just like she is. And while you may have had mentors and spiritual guides, much of life is a process you experience for yourself. In the 21ST century, women and men effectively have equal opportunities to education and resources that teach them soft and hard skills and leadership development. The skills she uses as the department manager are the same skills needed in a marriage. The skills he uses as principal of an elementary school are the same ones needed in marriage. The customer service skills of front-line employees are the same human relation skills needed in marriage. Men and women can only know what they know based on what they have been taught or have allowed themselves to learn.

Men are not built with a microchip that comes pre-loaded with how to be a man. Being a man is a daily process of growth. And if you have (or desire) a wife in your life, then her job as a helpmeet is to support your sustained growth into being a better man. Your job is to do the same for her. Marriage is a partnership in which you both learn and grow together by teaching and supporting each other. Many men are hurt from failed relationships or abusive pasts that date back to childhood, and as a result have developed insecurities, complexes, and stark ways of seeing the world. Women are not the only abused group of humans in our society. Short of feeling constrained to an abusive relationship, your wife's job is to love you through your healing process. Your job is to allow her to love you through it as you love her through her healing process as well.

When the heir to the throne is born, he is declared heir to the throne. Elders and leaders mentor and educate the lad into what they hope will be a great heir. In spite of the lad's shortsightedness, rambunctiousness, or misbehavior, they still know and treat him as the heir. The formative years of the heir may indicate to the mentors that this heir will be a good king or a bad king, but the question is never "is he the future king?" He is always the future king. Similarly, so is being a man. The great misnomer is that you have to learn to be a man. The truth is you are a man—you only have to learn how to be a great one.

#4 Father Replacement

I maintain a belief that many women are looking for a man to be their father through the title and role of husband. Historical factors, traditionalism, and the social construct support this belief. We have observed many traditional American weddings wherein the father walks his daughter down the aisle and hands her to the husband to be. The symbolism reflects a transfer of responsibility from father to husband, which is easily interpreted with an expectation of meeting or exceeding the standard set forth by her father. Women, therefore, tend to class their husband as synonymous to the father they had, never had, or desired, making fatherhood to husband inextricably linked. The high expectation for men to be in the know partly comes from the inherent process of a husband replacing the male figure of father in a woman's life.

Unfortunately, father replacement is problematic in the following way. A woman's expectation for a man to enter her life being well aware of how to treat a woman, be decisive, and manage the relationship is an expectation based on the image often modeled after the father. The fallacy in this expectation is that the daughter was not the father's wife. The daughter experienced the father or male figure as a child and not as her mother (the father's wife), which means the child was not privy to the developmental process of the father. The wife would have been the one directly experiencing and enduring the father's faults or areas that needed improvement as they both worked together to build one another as father and mother/husband and wife. What the child received would have been the result of the father going through the process with his wife.

If a daughter grows into adulthood expecting a man to be in the know as her father was, she mistakes her childhood role for being her father's wife, thereby robbing her future husband of the rightful opportunity to grow and develop. In other words, the child, now an adult woman, must go through the process with her spouse in order to help him grow into the father she experienced as a child (considering it was an appropriate and healthy experience). He cannot become the man her father was if she's not willing to put in the work as the woman by his side as her mother had endured with her father. There is a looming expectation for men to come to the table prepared, oftentimes expected to placate and acquiesce as a father may have done to his daughter. To the contrary, I

Corinthians 13:11 does not speak to just the male gender when it says, "*When I was a child, I spake as a child, I understood as a child, I thought as a child: but when I became a man, I put away childish things.*" The word *man* does not preclude women from the necessity of growth discussed by the author of that biblical passage. A woman must also put away the speaking, understanding, and thinking as a child, mature into adult/womanhood, and put away childish things.

While she was a child, observing Daddy (or a male figure), so were you. Meaning, you are no more in the know of how to lead. You have not made your mistakes with your wife yet (nor she with you), or come to understand areas that need development for the purpose and prosperity of your marriage. Because a parent, for the most part, directs the movement of children, women are primed to receiving directives, which comes with a high expectation for men to know what they are doing. However, male children have also experienced their father or male figure being "in the know" and directing their movements. So, here again we must acknowledge that you were a child and you were not your mother's husband growing and learning with her as husband and father. Subsequently, you are relatively ignorant, and she is relatively ignorant with an expectation for you to know and lead in your ignorance.

I also believe the first man a woman ever loves is her father, which means her identity is also tied to the relationship she has with him. This can potentially make for a contentious future if she never fell in love with him. She may never come to fall in love with him because 1) her father is absent (absenteeism), 2) her father is present but neglectful (poor parenting), or 3) her father is present and she is misguided by her own motives (rebellious child). The energy of love is amassed from our innate, original design as beings created to care, share, and love. Even if she never falls in love with her father, the amassed energy and expectation of love must be expressed. The amassed energy will either *disperse*, which seems like a healthier option, or *combust* in toxicity. There are multiple yet divergent roads in how the energy is expressed; but they eventually merge back into one path.

On one road, the amassed energy to love a man is dispersed to a boyfriend or husband in her attempt to find a man to "replace" the father that she originally wanted to fall in love with. This may seem like a healthier approach, but it is not a solution. In this approach, her desire for her significant other to meet her fatherly need is a very delicate matter. The husband's failure to uphold this role can be devastating to her emotional welfare and eventually lead to combustion of the energy she has amassed.

On another road, the amassed energy to love may become erratic as she engages in unhealthy ways to express this energy. Unhealthy behavior may include promiscuity, anger management issues, or narcissistic behavior. She wants to love but doesn't know how to do so in a constructive, meaningful way. She may ebb and flow between behaviors that disperse and combust the energy. Nonetheless, she is emotionally unstable in this state of mind.

The singular path women must come to is exonerating men from being the replacement of their father. While most women inevitably seek a man to express the full love of copulation and family, she does so with the initial building blocks of the love she has amassed for her first love, her father. She may or may not be aware of this dynamic in her life, especially if she has yet to express this love. The initial role of the father in having a daughter in love with him was to show her how to love herself. This is a deficit she must repair by understanding that in the absence of her father, her first love becomes herself. She cannot love a man in a healthy, parallel relationship if she does not disperse the love for her father unto herself first. As a husband, you can aid in the process of healing, but our healing is always our individual responsibility.

Being the replacement of her father is not a fair task for any man. But both men and women create emotional expectations of one another based on the relationship they have had with their parents, or lack thereof. It's a catch-22. Your role as a husband is to be the support she needs. But it's important to do that in the context of husband, and not be held to the obligation or standard of her father. You are not her father. You are your own person with your own set of experiences and expectations who was once a child, just like her, looking up to parental leadership. Parental leadership is not usually a partnership between child and parent. Some people will say that as a husband you should be everything she needs, which means if she needs you to fill the void of something not provided by her father, then you are responsible for that as well. I advise strong caution against that because you may find yourself responsible for an emotional pain that she needs to resolve on her own. It is not your job to fill the void; it is your job to wisely encourage and be supportive. Trying to be her source of healing in the fatherhood to husband exchange is a responsibility that may easily outweigh you depending on the depth of her trauma or expectations. She has a responsibility to herself and the marriage to tackle that issue as you have the same responsibility to yourself and the marriage.

#5 Men Cry Too: Showing Emotions & Vulnerability

Men are not tough-skinned individuals who have a limited range of emotions and routine actions. Men share the same qualities in the same depth, scope and breadth as women. For example, there's a tendency to believe women are more prone than men to being nurturers. People tend to believe this because the woman gives birth. The fact is men can be nurturers and not all mothers have a nurturing personality. I do not mean this as a point of generalization to include men who are nurturers as outliers. I mean that in an everyday context, men's personality type and character are equally prone to being nurturing, comforting, affectionate, compassionate, gentle, thoughtful, loving, easygoing, passionate, sensitive, and faithful, just to name a few. If you do not already portray these traits and more, know you are capable. Your gender does not preclude you from any trait or dictate the quality of the traits you possess.

The truth is that men are very emotional, as are all human beings. The problem is what do we do with that emotion? I have witnessed mothers telling their sons to stop crying because boys are not supposed to cry. Crying is cathartic. It helps to release the strong emotions of whatever is physically or psychologically causing those emotions. But when the son is told that boys do not cry, what then does he do with that emotion? He holds on to it. And with further incidents that occur in which he is told that it is not okay for him to emote, he continues to store up those feelings until he violently lashes out or emotionally retreats.

We see this play out in marriages frequently. The man, in his role of being a "real" man, has to find a way to remain logical (as opposed to being emotional), find a way to not be bothered by inconveniences, and remain firm and strong in his display of manhood. The dark side to this unhealthy socialization of boys into manhood is the hypermasculinity it creates. Hypermasculinity leads to chauvinism and dominating behaviors over women in order to always prove that the man is a "real" man. Moreover, many men find themselves at a spilling point that lands them in angry confrontations with their spouse or other people from the buildup of suppressed emotions.

How have men been traditionally taught to deal with their emotions through violence? In patriarchal societies, James Gilligan's book *Preventing Violence* (2001) discusses how "shame" is a social cause of violence. "Men are shamed for not being violent enough (called cowards or even shot as deserters), and are more honored the more violent they are (with medals, promotions, titles, and estates)—violence for men is a successful strategy. Women, however, are shamed for being too active and aggressive (called bitches or unfeminine) and honored for being passive and submissive—violence is much less likely to protect them against shame" (pp. 38-39).

The challenge is that some women box men into caveman roles of brawn and brute and do not allow men to evolve in other areas of their personality. You are pigeonholed as provider, protector, sexually-charged beings, and sexual objects. For example, my wife at the time was challenged in being affectionate with me. The fallout from this issue was immense because I am a very affectionate man who likes to communicate through touch. I like to hug, hold hands, wrestle, tickle, be playful, and have that reciprocated. However, she never really bought in to the idea of it all. She once said to me, "I never knew men liked stuff like that," a reflection of her upbringing, no doubt. In this situation, I had been boxed into being one thing. Ironically, the Women's Suffrage Movement/Feminism is one big showdown to prove women are not just one thing.

Showing emotions and being vulnerable to your spouse should not come with a rejection of who you are. And being a man does not eliminate any trait from being a dominant component of your personality. The confusion lies in the conflation of feminine traits, masculine traits, and the assignment of gender roles. This will be further discussed in a future section on roles vs. tasks.

Your growth into greatness as a man will require you to show emotions. It is okay to express to your spouse that you are saddened, bothered, troubled in spirit, concerned, angry (but sin not), flustered, fearful, experiencing feelings of inadequacy, or whatever else that are normal human emotions. It is her job to listen, remind you that you were not created with a spirit of fear, but of "love, power, and a sound mind" (2 Timothy 1:7), to encourage, uplift and pray you through those emotions. As a husband, you should not have to tackle these emotions on your own—too often we believe we have to because that is part of what being a man is. You also share the same responsibility to your wife. Your job is to remind her of who she is, encourage, uplift, and pray her through the moments when the human emotions try to overtake her. Neither of you are weak for being human. Being human is already a weakened state of existence. In fact, your ability to be transparent and vulnerable in these moments is a display of strength.

#6 Roles vs. Tasks

The social conversation proposes a handful of concrete things as definitive for a man or woman to do. They have become gender roles forged in the fire of tradition. To qualify the duty of a man or woman, the term "real" becomes affixed. For example, a *real* man is supposed to pump gas. A *real* woman is supposed to provide a home cooked meal. A *real* man is supposed to take out the garbage, open doors, pull out chairs, fix things around the house, service the car, and do yard work, to name a few. Also, the role of a man is to pay for dates, pay for her upkeep (hair, nails, and clothes), and pay bills. It is a combination of chivalry and household and financial duties. Roles are not defined by tasks. By confusing roles with tasks, many people become taskmasters in their expectations of their significant other.

I do not take out the garbage because I am the man. I take out the garbage because I believe in a clean home, and a clean environment helps to keep the mind organized. She does not wash clothes because a woman is supposed to wash clothes, but because the service rendered is from a space of caring for her spouse, and quite simply, it is a necessity for a clean environment. Task performance ought to be routine, responsible adult behavior.

Role, on the other hand, is more fundamental and suited to our intrinsic values that reflect how we lead, influence, build, mentor, coach, and promote the enterprise of the relationship. That is very different from cutting the grass or washing dishes. You can hire someone to do those tasks. But you cannot hire someone to fill your role.

I have developed a simple rubric for determining whether a matter is a task or role. If I can pay someone to do it, then it is a task. If a maid can be paid to do household chores; if a chef can be paid to prepare meals; if a butler can be paid to serve you; if a handyman can be paid to fix household items; if a driver can be paid to transport you; and if a gardener and lawn care company can be paid to service your landscaping, then it is a task. **The role of a man cannot be categorized as an expense.** The butler cannot be paid to pillow talk with your wife. The maid cannot be paid to provide words of encouragement. The handyman cannot be paid to buy gifts that commemorate milestones in the marriage. Tasks are not the role of a man. In fact, most tasks can be completed by any gender. Single men and women complete these tasks on their own all the time. Somehow, in the middle of forming a union, people decide to introduce task-oriented social norms that create misguided expectations.

In knowing that the role of a man or woman speaks to the deeper intrinsic values of the relationship, tasks become inconsequential and unassigned to gender. She can take out the garbage and you can do laundry. You can do it together; she can wash, you can fold; or you can wash and fold. Notwithstanding, after long periods of managing certain responsibilities it becomes expected for the person to continue completing that task within the relationship. However, the role of a man or the woman is not to be defined by the task. Scott Delman expounds on the difference in his write-up, *Tasks vs. Role: Bringing Home The Bacon*[3]**.** He defines *task* as a "piece of work" assigned or done as part of one's duties and *role* as "the actions and activities assigned to or required or expected of a person or group." Delman pinpoints role as understanding the standards of the organization (in this case marriage) that makes the person aware of what optimum performance looks like and tasks as a piece of work that must be completed with no higher order objective attached to it. In this space of defining tasks versus roles, you find many men unsure of what they ought to be to a woman. They want to have a role, but the communication about "what you bring to the table" is overwhelmingly task-oriented. It is doublespeak that both men and women often project onto each other.

#7 Gender vs. Masculine and Feminine Traits

Gender and traits are intermingled in the same way we confuse tasks and roles because gender and traits are notoriously used as a rationale to uphold assigning tasks and roles. This occurs when the traits are assigned to a gender (almost exclusively), thereby setting the stage as to why a task should be completed by that gender. If the

3 http://www.watercoolerwisdom.com/newsletters/col2/Tasks-vs-Role_Bringing-Home-The-Bacon.pdf

trait is feminine, then the task is assigned to the woman; if the trait is masculine, then the task is assigned to the man. For example, a feminine trait is nurturer, which leads many people to believe that childrearing is largely the duty of the woman. As a result, men are largely perceived as not nurturing. Similarly, leadership is viewed as a masculine trait, which leads many to see being head of state as largely a man's responsibility. As a result, women are largely viewed as unfit to lead, especially in a large capacity. The mistake is that feminine traits are assigned to women and masculine traits are assigned to men in a way that makes it almost exclusive to that gender. This is inaccurate. Masculine and feminine traits are behavioral qualities that stem from our personalities, impacted by our socialization process, and expressed by both men and women.

Masculine traits include	Feminine traits include
Provider	Nurturer/Caretaker
Protector	Social
Leader	Quiet (Seen and Not Heard)
Spatial	Verbal
Independent	Dependent
Assertive	Passive
Appeals to Logic	Appeals to Emotion
Dominant/Aggressive	Gentle/Patient
Disciplined	Carefree
Violent	Submissive
Authoritative	Tactful

Traits are a way of understanding and reflecting our personality types. Femininity is not solely female, nor is masculinity solely male. Mother Nature and Father Time gender assignment reflects its characteristics, not so much maleness or femaleness. Mother Nature gives life, bears fruits, and provides water. We are defining Mother Nature as a nurturer. In essence, Mother Nature takes care of us as a mother does a child. Father Time is absolute, consistent, disciplined, and unchanging. In essence, Father Time provides safety and assurance in its consistency. We are defining Father Time as a leader. But at closer examination, Mother Nature and Father Time share more traits (characteristics) in common than differences. Mother Nature consistently raises the sun in the East, has violent storms, and can be assertive as a concrete rose. Father Time can be patient (because all things happen in due time), it quietly passes, and while it waits for no one, allows you to manage it to your liking.

I know, as you might, men who are not fixtures of taking charge, dominating, and being more inclined to appeal to logic and likewise, women who are not passive, quiet, and submissive in their presentation. In fact, I know a number of men who are empathetic, quiet, and seemingly passive at times. I also know men who are assertive, action-oriented, and protective. Likewise, we know women whose personalities encapsulate a combination of masculine and feminine traits. This is not a case for gender fluidity. I am simply contending that assignment of gender to trait, which upholds the assignment of tasks, is another misnomer that boxes men and women into social constructs that invariably result in conflict.

#8 Relationship/Marriage Failure is the Man's Fault

I was invited to sit on a relationship panel in Nassau, Bahamas by Transformation and Transition Strategist Simmone L. Bowe. The panel featured some of Nassau's most eloquent and recognized community members, who spoke with depth on the good, the bad, and the ugly of relationships. During the event, co-host DJ Epic made an incredible point about the perception of manhood versus womanhood. A female panel member was discussing the definition of a man and the importance of men to "step up to the plate." She pointed out that being insecure as a man was not a manly trait. DJ Epic asked at what point is a man no longer a man? She replied that a man who is still working on his self-image, heavily reliant on a woman taking care of him, or without a stable job are signs of him not being a man. DJ Epic then asked at what point is a woman not a woman? After she fumbled around with the answer, in epic fashion, DJ Epic solidified his point, concluding that the tendency amongst men and women is that at no point, in spite of her insecurities, lack of self-worth, or financial dependency is a woman not considered a woman.

Note the conundrum. The perception of women as always being a woman derives from the religious, political, economic, and historically supported systems that box women into the feminine traits of submissive, dependent, and incapable of leading and providing for herself (or a man). Therefore, a woman is always second to a man, and always in need of provision and protection by a man. At the moment a man falls below the ability to provide and protect for a woman, he is then also seen as less than a man, and may be further categorized as feminine. Again, we see the contextualization of traits (dependent) assigned to gender (female), and gender assigned to the tasks (operate in an understanding as second to a man).

Nonetheless, the double standard pointed out by DJ Epic shined light on the prevailing idea that the failure of relationships, specifically marriages, is largely the fault of the husband. Notwithstanding some great offense by the wife such as adultery, our society permits and anticipates women as the victims of men who were not man enough and did not know how to love and cherish his wife. Overwhelmingly, the religious perspectives of people who adopt the belief that the man is the head of household also view the failure of the marriage as a failure of headship or leadership.

The expectation of headship also brings into play the expectation to know, the maturity to father your wife, be emotionally mature, and assume accountability for every area of your marriage. In effect, almost by definition of being a man, men are expected to be more mature and accountable than their female counterparts. Following this line of thinking, it is almost inevitably the case that the actions or inactions of husbands are identified as the cause of marital breakdowns. On the other hand, society feeds us that women, considered the nurturing and more caring of the sexes, are by default good people. Continuing to follow this line of thinking leads to another great misnomer inherent to many women's thinking. There is a tendency to believe that women instinctively know how to be good wives by default of being a woman, similarly to how they instinctively know how to be mothers.

That is false. Women, by default, are not good wives in the same manner men as the husband, by default, are not the cause of breakdowns in romantic relationships. Husbands and wives must learn how to be good spouses to each other. Two consenting adults are equally responsible for the success of the marriage and both will most likely be responsible for any unfortunate demise. A wife is capable of destroying her marriage no differently from the ability of a husband to do the same.

However, our Western society and many other cultures have accepted this conclusion regarding relationships because the woman plays possum in this cyclical and divisive display of power dynamics. The woman is not at all second to the man. (She knows that, but pretends to not know and allows the man to think he has all, if not most, of the power; men tend to not want to know because they view her equality as a loss of power.) She derives power from the power base of men by holding them accountable to their own hegemonic and patriarchal approaches found in their masculine traits. In effect, she taps into masculinity to hold him responsible for his own masculinity. In other words, she leads the charge in holding him accountable to lead, and when he does not, she turns him over to the larger society to be chastised as feminine. Her power is further derived in that she is able to be both feminine and masculine with less prejudice; meanwhile, a man is expected to usually be masculine.

#9 Doing Right by Her Doesn't Mean She'll Stay with You

Jonathan was faithful to her. He assisted her through engineering school by taking on the bulk of the household chores, tending to their two children, and managing the finances. He and his wife were well known amongst their friends and the church community. She worked part-time and found herself mostly committed to her studies. He knew how important her academics and career were to her. Upon completion of her degree, she landed a full-time job with a significant salary. The great news was bittersweet. As her life was reaching a high point, she revealed to him that she had been in an affair for nearly two years and had finally decided that she wanted to be with her lover permanently. Jonathan was devastated as she revealed the details of her affair and demanded a divorce immediately. Taken by surprise, he asked what he had done to deserve this. She informed him that he had not done anything wrong per se, but she wanted more out of life, including more fun, more experiences, and something altogether different. The emotional toll of a highly stressful divorce led Jonathan to losing his job and going broke. He lost weight, sank into depression, and could not hold down a steady job for a couple years. Over the years he had to consistently endure seeing his ex-wife and his children under another roof with her new husband. While Jonathan no doubt made mistakes during the marriage, overall, he was a committed husband and father who married young and never considered that one day, in spite of his best intentions for his family and their future, he would be facing divorce.

There are many men who enter marriage with faithful, caring, submissive, and open-minded intentions. However, your best intentions toward your wife to be spiritually, emotionally, and physically supportive, including the traditional expectations of provider and protector, being a prayerful man, and even having great financial stability does not guarantee a long-lasting, healthy relationship.

Many, if not most men want healthy, fulfilling relationships, just like many/most women do. Nonetheless, what is the guarantee that if you do right by her that she will do right by you? Unfortunately, we hear plenty of one-sided stories of men as the cause of failed relationships. If the divorce rate is 50 percent, which means for every hundred couples marrying that 50 couples are divorcing, then the cause of marital failure cannot be the predominant fault of men alone. There are people who believe planet Earth is the only inhabited planet in the universe. If the mathematical formula allows for humans to exist on Earth, then by the same possibility we exist, other life forms exist on other planets throughout the solar system. Likewise, men cannot be the only existing cause of relationship failure. There are other life forms in the marriage.

Men and women, both young adult and older, repeatedly hear stories about the adulterous affairs of men and their mistreatment of women. As a result, the perception is that men tend to practice infidelity much more frequently than women. According to the trainer of the Miami-Dade County parenting class, infidelity in marriage is generally 50/50. The trainer expounded that married people statistically engaged in extra-marital affairs with other married people. In other words, married women statistically cheat equal to the number of married men, because they are cheating with each other.

This is an important statistic to digest because the social conversation continuously places women as victims when in fact they are fully capable of being equally responsible for the breakdown in marriages. Women are human beings, and do human things. Infidelity, for example, is a human thing, not a male thing.

#10 Men Are from Mars, Women Are from Venus

Probably the most diabolical of all the misnomers is the belief that men and women want diametrically different things in life and in relationships. Yet, here we are, both on planet Earth, procreating and recreating together. I know the adage "men are from Mars and women are from Venus" is intended to show how differently we think, experience the world, and draw conclusions about the world. But conflict is inherent to its claim as opposed to recognizing men and women as a continuum of each other. But as mentioned before, neither men nor women are monolithic groups of genders. The fact is that men and women both want healthy, productive, and supportive relationships. The question is, how do we work together to achieve it? I believe the starting point is acknowledging that we are both, oftentimes, coming from the same emotional space of expectations.

Men and women are from where they are socialized. Upon marriage, you bring the weight of the other person's life into yours, inclusive of their physical, emotional, and spiritual selves:

- Physical items include your physical presence, clothing, furniture, pictures, and pets. Later in the marriage it may include in-laws and children.
- Emotional items include pets and pet peeves, personality type, leadership and management styles, and problem-solving skills.
- Spiritual items include core values that shape the foundation of the person, the absolute most important things to the individual that consciously and subconsciously guides their daily actions and ways of seeing the world. They are often built on religious or spiritual beliefs and lived experiences.

Venus and Mars imply that we are worlds apart in our thinking and behavior, when in fact we are not. Men and women procreate in order to replenish the Earth with life. In spite of the misunderstandings, misconceptions, and misrepresentations that men and women have of each other, they somehow still find a way to come together long enough to create new life. We cannot be that different if our togetherness makes the biggest difference.

#11 Love and Respect

The notion that men ought to love their wives and women ought to respect their husbands is largely underpinned by Ephesians 5:33, which says, "Nevertheless let every one of you in particular so love his wife even as himself; and the wife see that she reverences her husband." While there is a level of truth to it, we should investigate another thought process.

Above all, no matter what the state of any relationship is, it is normal for the human being to demand their "respect," even if they are not loved or liked. A common saying is, "You don't have to like me, but you will respect me." In other words, respect is the demand for the acknowledgement of an individual's power and autonomy of "self." The "self," front and center, wants to ensure certain thresholds of the person's identity are not overstepped, usurped, or in other words, "disrespected." Simply put, the "self" we speak of is the man's ego.

A husband's demand or expectation to be respected is linked to his social normative views of his sense of power and identity, wherein, as head or leader, he expects to have a certain level of control over the marriage. The slippery slope is when the ego becomes consumed with pride. Furthermore, stating the husband should be respected implies the woman does not have the same level of responsibility toward loving her husband. In this arrangement, love is a secondary matter; rather, she is to place his authority and autonomy as a primary focus.

Next, love, on the other hand, covers a multitude of faults (1 Peter 4:8). By focusing on the wife's need for love, we suggest to the man to be flexible, patient, and tender toward her. Unfortunately, because loving the woman appeases the emotionality of the woman, we in turn discount the emotions of the man, thereby discounting his need for love. Respect, on the other hand, promotes the authority and autonomy of the man, therefore the ego of the man. It reminds me of a parent-child or teacher-student relationship, in which the parent or teacher is the authoritative figure that demands respect from the children, while the children are in need of comfort and shelter, therefore in need of love. It is a one-way transaction that paints an incomplete picture.

Lastly, the concept of man-love-wife and wife-respect-husband is further problematic because it does not recognize the respect the woman also needs, thereby failing to recognize and acknowledge her sense of self, authority, and autonomy within the marriage. In failing to do so, we also hold her less accountable for the outcome of the relationship.

She is perceived as less accountable because she is seen as having less authority and autonomy than her husband. Her identity is also subsumed into his. Therefore, there is less of a need for her recognition. This imbalance in perceiving the husband as having the greater power and autonomy shifts a greater burden onto him as ultimately being more responsible for the success or failure of the marriage. This lay of the land provides the right atmosphere for conflict. It conceptually pits husbands and wives against each other as they each take turns vying for love and respect.

I implore you to understand that respect is found in love; love is not necessarily found in respect. Both husband and wife desire and need to be loved, and in the space of love created within the relationship, respect is also expected to be expressed by both parties equally. We have to properly position love. Love bears all things, believes all things, and hopes all things (1 Corinthians 3:7). God is love (1 John 4:8). Love is all encompassing. Husbands need love; wives need love; and in the process, they both need equal acknowledgement of their authority, autonomy, and identity from each other.

#12 Happy Wife, Happy Life:

A Matter of Individualism vs. Collectivism Part 1

The idiom "happy wife, happy life" placates the emotionality of women and lessens her accountability. It also pivots women into a position of power because it is a standard determined by her, met by him, and assessed by her—a quid quo pro that promises to keep you happy, if you keep her happy. Where "respect" recognized his authority and autonomy and love catered to her emotional appeal, "happy wife, happy life" now forces him to surrender his authority for her assurance. This process runs in one direction: her happiness leads to his happiness. But what if it does not lead to his happiness? Does he need to do a better job at making her happy? No part of the process makes her accountable for **not** making him happy.

Ultimately, "happy wife, happy life" is a lopsided scale that places a larger burden on the man, and if failed, is easily concluded as a need for him to more effectively meet her needs. Fortunately, because she is unhappy does not mean you have not done your part to make her happy. Some women are just unhappy individuals with their own personal battles to overcome before they can appreciate and reciprocate happiness. Similarly, your unresolved or mismanaged personal battles will prevent you from properly internalizing the ways in which your wife has reciprocated.

Part 2

Additionally, some women are stuck between collectivism and individualism, and do not know how to reconcile the two. Collectivism is a community-centered mindset. On the other hand, individualism is self-centered and self-promoting. I refer to this individualistic mentality as centerfolding, placing one's self *as* the center of the relationship.

The engrained socialized belief that upholds women as the weaker sex leads to female individualism, a me-first mindset as a measure of protection against their vulnerabilities. Female individualism echoes: provide for me, protect me, take care of me, uplift me, support me, value me, and so on. At face value, there is absolutely nothing wrong with these expectations. However, when these expectations are established as self-centered ideals, it strongly communicates an "all about me" attitude. In other words, it is a sustained belief in the "happy wife, happy life" notion.

On the flip side, men are expected to practice collectivism toward women, in which he embraces the woman into his community and willingly facilitates provision and protection (the perceived role of a "real" man). Added to the narrative that women are the victims of our society, in the belief that they are weaker, you get an even more entrenched mentality that supports the narrative that her protection and livelihood are more critical than her male counterpart. All of this happens while concurrently declaring the man as having headship, leadership, and authority over the marriage.

As the primary entity beholden to happiness, female individualism works well with male collectivism as long as his headship and autonomy is steered toward her. Again, observe the power dynamics. Her individualism controls his collectivism while he is simultaneously told he is the leader. What is he truly leading? In reality, I observe this as a feminist pushback to a male-dominated world of hegemony. While I understand the women's core value of protection against her "weaknesses," the pushback is misguided when applied without acknowledging that most men are not rich, powerful beings that dominate the lives of women. As a result, many men also see female individualism as a type of misandry of gynocentrism.

Most men, like most women in America, are middle class individuals stuck in the fight for access and upward mobility against a socio-economic system that usually results in the rich getting richer and the poor getting poorer. The reality is even starker when you look at the economic plight of most men and women around the world. The sleight of hand purported by the rich and wealthy is to make the issues of classism appear as an issue of racism and genderism. As long as the underclass remains fixated on issues of race and gender, the runway is clear for capitalistic oligarchs to take off to higher monetary heights.

Furthermore, female individualism does not speak inclusively or collectively of the man. In the social conversation, the individualistic-minded woman presents a one-sided expectation in which the man is a tool of provision and protection with her as the centerfold of his world. On the other hand, the communal-minded conversation utilizes the *We* as the centerfold of the relationship: we provide for each other; we protect each other; we take care of each other; we love each other; we support each other; we uplift each other. Oneness is oneness.

I firmly believe that when we move away from the romanticized Eurocentric ideals that place individualism and capitalism at the forefront, and return to our communal roots of the *We* mentality, we will see much better results in the transaction of love and life that upholds the mantra "happy we, happy me," placing communal values in the forefront and individualism to the background.

Men employ the same tactics of centerfolding by maintaining an individualistic mentality that says the relationship centers around their role as man, provider, protect, head of household, and breadwinner. Such patriarchal beliefs result in hypermasculinity. And conflict ensues between two people attempting to centerfold the relationship.

THE META-VALUES OF THE BIBLE

CHAPTER 4

You would think churchgoers would get marriage "right." But that point of view is a fallacy often taken on by both churchgoers and non-churchgoers. Churchgoers do not have an upper hand on marriage. In fact, I have observed an undue pressure on relationships to "get it right" because they are churchgoers. It is a pressure that many couples cannot live up to for reasons such as conflicting messages in the church, demonization of members, and poor examples set by the leadership. I personally had to learn to refrain from this thinking after watching my marriage lose both of its engines, crash, and burn. Churchgoers sometimes also undergo an identity crisis as they grow to 1) know who they are as spiritual and earthly creatures versus 2) who the church says they are as parishioners.

Nonetheless, whether you are an atheist, agnostic, or Holy Ghost-filled, tambourine-playing saint, the social norms of most societies are established through some form of a religious dogma, which in turn drives our socialization process and the ways in which we interact as a society. Religion serves as the foundation of our moral and social beliefs. It also underpins our values to validate and facilitate the social order of what is right or wrong, good or evil, acceptable and unacceptable, and decent and indecent. As a result, religious dogma informs our social norms, impacting how rules and legislation are crafted, which further impacts the way organizations are formed. Many of our beliefs or philosophy on the role of men and women are largely derived from our religious teachings and lived and historical experiences. This makes the Bible, the Quran, and religious texts in general an important part of the discussion of marriage.

The Church does not insulate married couples from marital problems such as infidelity, domestic abuse, or divorce. Yet it seems that so many of the messages in Christian churches are about marital relationships. It is as if the church system serves as an assembly line for marriages in both putting them together and sometimes tearing them apart. The storyline of marriage throughout the Christian church can largely be attributed to the Bible itself, which metaphorically describes the relationship between Christ and His followers as husband and wife. Yet neither the leading character of the New Testament, Jesus Christ, nor one of its foremost contributors, Apostle Paul, are recorded in the Bible as being married.

JESUS CHRIST & APOSTLE PAUL

The Bible does not record Jesus Christ as having much to say about marriage beyond his admonishment to the Pharisees who queried him about divorce in Matthew 19:1-12. In this chapter, Jesus Christ spoke about husband and wife becoming one flesh; proclaimed fornication as the only cause for divorce; alluded that the hardened hearts of men toward their wives was a substandard reason for divorce; and emphatically protested against divorce, referring to remarriage of divorcees as an adulterous act. Take note that in this day and age, second marriages are not uncommon nor viewed as adulterous. Jesus Christ also implied that marriage was not for everyone because some people were called to serve as eunuchs for the sake of ministry. Catholic priests and nuns may be considered ministerial eunuchs.

Outside of Jesus Christ's death, burial, and resurrection, Apostle Paul is arguably the most prolific contributor of the New Testament. Many denominations are built on the words of Apostle Paul, whose writing has helped to shape gender roles and has inadvertently been used to establish patriarchal hierarchy. Yet, Apostle Paul concluded marriage was not necessary for him because of his gift of chastity (1 Corinthians 7:1–7). As a point of personal order, I take two types of advice from others with a heavy grain of salt: marriage and parenting. I am not asserting that God cannot speak through whomever He chooses—He once spoke through a donkey (Numbers 22:28)—however, it is peculiar that the foremost leading authorities on the biblical underpinnings of marriage and the rhetoric that most Christian people use as foundational social norms stem from individuals who may not have ever been married. I find that thought provoking, but, in truth, I do not find it incompatible.

As the Christ of God, Jesus' mission was to be the sacrificial lamb to redeem mankind back unto God. The relationship that Jesus had with God provided Him spiritual insight on all subject matters. However, I am more curious, and in some ways, guarded of Apostle Paul's beliefs because he fulfilled a different role than that of Jesus Christ. Apostle Paul represented the redemptive process accessible to mankind in a world post Christ's death, burial, resurrection, and ascension. The redemptive process is that individuals "not be conformed to this world: but be ye transformed by the renewing of your mind, that ye may prove what is that good, and acceptable, and perfect, will of God" (Romans 12:2).

However, the process of redemption and deepening one's spirituality occurs within the scope of a person's lived and historical experiences, which means that Saul's transformation to Apostle Paul could have only occurred in the context of his socialization. This context includes his interactions and perception of women. I am not a farmer and I have never worked within the field of producing crops. It is extremely unlikely that I will ascertain spiritual enlightenment regarding farming to guide farmers on farming. However, I am a social scientist that has extensive experience as a husband, father, and church leader with impactful experiences in those spaces. As such, my lived and historical experiences are the backdrop of my spiritual revelations and maturation. As such, what then were Apostle Paul's lived and historical experiences that brought him to his spiritual enlightenment regarding marriage?

With this in mind, we can understand the limitations of Apostle Paul's enlightenment. While the process of spiritual growth is without limits, spiritual revelations are set to our personal experiences in a particular place and time. The number of people who may adopt the enlightenment into their lives does not override the limitations of the messenger.

CONFLICTING MESSAGES

Church teachings promoted by various denominations reveal a pattern of contrasting messages found throughout the Bible, particularly on marriages and the role of men and women in society. For example, some churches teach women are relegated to the home (Titus 2:5), while other churches point to the entrepreneurialism of women (Proverbs 31). The teaching that a woman should not teach/preach (1 Timothy 2:12) and remain silent in church (1 Corinthians 14:34) has a way of spilling over into the marriage as to how a woman should behave in general, i.e. seen and not heard. On the other hand, some churches embrace women in leadership and ministerial work as seen in Acts 18:26 and John 20:18. Another important distinction is that some denominations contend the Old Testament is obsolete in light of the New Testament.

On another note, slave owners in the United States of America used the Bible to justify the master-slave relationship (Colossians 3:22); however, rewrites and updated versions of the Bible have changed several words, including the word "slavery" to "servants." (I do not think slave owners from 200-400 years ago would have found it convenient to translate "slaves" to "servants.") Ultimately, for almost every major claim asserted by one Scripture you can find a contrasting Scripture. The ping-pong of hermeneutics is divisive as people grapple over details and misinformation.

META-VALUES OF THE BIBLE

How do we make sense of it all now that we have established the Bible can at times appear contradictory, is used by religious leaders to serve their institutional purpose, and has fostered disagreement as evidenced by the numerous religions and denominations that exist? How do we establish order in ourselves and in our lives when so much contradiction encircles us? We can clarify all of the contrasting interpretations, Scriptures, and presuppositions throughout the Bible by understanding the main ideas and universal theme throughout the Bible. I define the Bible as **a book of transcending human-interest stories that model how good overcomes evil and love overcomes hate through obedience, selflessness, and great undertakings of the human spirit guided by a force greater than itself. The Bible is value-added to our process of spirituality.**

Value speaks to the worth, merit, and importance of something. Meta takes the analysis of the subject matter to a deeper and sometimes more abstract level in order to formulate a greater understanding of the subject. Meta-value is therefore understanding the deeper and overarching principle that guides our subject matter: the role of a man in loving and leading. In addition to everything purported throughout the social conversation, as mentioned before, religious teachings are the starting place for much of the held views on the role of men and women.

Accordingly, the subject matter has to be addressed using the Bible. However, biblical text is only a starting point, which is why we can most safely look at the overarching message or meta-values of Scripture and not the minutiae provided in the text. God did not disappear after the Book of Revelations to no longer provide mankind further instructions on holy living.

My synthesis of the Bible identifies four overarching themes or meta-values: 1) Leadership, 2) Submission, 3) Provision and Protection, and 4) Relationship Building. My point of view on these topics is set apart in that I focus on the universal principles of the Bible in an effort to specifically resolve the conflicts between Scriptures that clearly show opposing viewpoints. My goal is to identify the most altruistic point or lesson being taught through these human-interest stories. From a birds-eye view of each story, we can walk away with a holistic view of the Bible that cuts through the confusion, allowing us to understand how the whole is greater than the sum of its parts. To focus on the variance between Scriptures, what I also call matters of minutiae, makes us susceptible to the little foxes that spoil the vine (Solomon 2:15) or the details where some say the devil is found. The following four meta-values of the Bible will help you overcome these conflicts and help align your thinking to a greater purpose as a man and husband with a higher order understanding of biblical text.

Leadership

The stories of the Bible are stories of leaders and leadership. Leadership is a spiritual, emotional, and physical process that requires focus, attentiveness, understanding, a willingness to support the success of others, and is done by example. Leadership is spiritual as it reflects your core values and perception of the world around you. It is also spiritual because it's built on the relationship you first have with yourself, which is an internal process. Leadership is emotional as it reflects your frame of mind, feelings, and approach toward managing life and resolving conflicts. Your emotions reflect to others the growth found within your spiritual self. Leadership is physical in that it is a conglomerate of executable skills that's learned over time, such as time management, verbal and written communication, financial management, and time management. Leaders influence their sphere to think and behave toward a certain goal.

I have not found the word leadership in the Bible. So from where do I ascertain leadership? What were Moses, Abraham, Samuel, Nehemiah, Jonah, Isaac, Jesus, the Disciples, and many more men in the Bible called to do? Each of their ministries called them to lead according to the purpose for which they were called in order to meet the needs of the people in their sphere of influence. Moreover, throughout the Bible we are continuously introduced to men in formal leadership positions such as kings, priests, and warriors and men of great influence in informal positions with wealth, gab, and insight to penetrate the establishment. We also witness the stories of maturation of young boys into adulthood throughout both the Old and New Testaments.

Many of the popular religious texts do not broadly capture the contributions of women. However, we see storylines that include the role of women throughout the Bible including Esther, Rahab, Ruth, Naomi, Rachel, Elizabeth (the mother of John the Baptist), Mary (wife of Joseph), and Mary Magdalene. Proverbs 31, a Scripture I fervently embrace, describes a woman with much means and influence in her circle with an ability to effectively communicate, manage, and execute. In other words, the Proverbs 31 woman was (or is) a leader along with the ministries in which other women in the Bible participated.

Also, the leadership style exhibited by many of these women and men of the Bible is referred to as servant-leadership. Leadership is fluid. It takes on necessary forms to find success for who and what it needs to lead. 1 Corinthians 3:16, which says, "Know ye not that ye are the temple of God, and that the Spirit of God dwelleth in you," was not a reminder to men only, but to all believers, women, children, and men alike. Leadership is also an act of submission by both parties in the leadership process. Effective leadership shares power, allows for the inclusion of varying perspectives, mentors others in an effort to build them up as leaders, resolves conflict in a respectful manner, and builds relationships with others for the betterment of the community.

The role of a husband is to lead. The role of a woman is to lead. More importantly, these men and women had purpose, vision, and a servant-leader mentality. The awesome thing about leadership is that everyone has the capacity to lead, men and women alike. Leadership and followship is a symbiotic relationship: leaders are followers and followers are leaders.

Submission

As you observe the leaders and the leadership espoused by the icons of the Bible, you will note a major trend of submission. Submission was not to an individual, but to a purpose declared through divine revelation. Moses had to deliver the Israelites from Pharaoh; Nehemiah had to build the wall; Daniel had to respond to the King's demands according to God's word; Jonah had to go to Nineveh; Joseph of the Old Testament had to be positioned for his family during the time of famine; Job had to undergo the direct attack of Lucifer in order to withstand and stand; John the Baptist had to pave the way for Jesus; Jesus Christ had to die on the cross; and Apostle Paul had to be knocked off his horse in order to know Jesus as the Christ. There are many more stories that showcase the submissive process undertaken in leadership.

Submission is a matter of humility. Humility is not the façade of meekness, and pride is not a braggadocious expression of self. Pride can be found in both; humility can be found in both. Humility, put simply, is a matter of obedience. Therefore, submission is a matter of obedience. Are you willing to do what your purpose asks of you?

Submission in marriage is not a wife-to-husband road map. The Scripture shows that men and women are called to submit to each other in the fear of God (Ephesians 5:21). The fear of God is the spotlight of the verse as it sets the barometer by which submission takes place. The submission part of leadership is overlooked because it is often interpreted as weakness while leadership appeals to strength. Emphatically, leadership is wisdom, and in wisdom is strength—the strength to move forward forcibly or the strength to retreat quietly. Ultimately, effective leaders undertake the process of submission.

Marriage is not a matter of fate and destiny, and the rest works itself out. Marriage requires submission to the process of learning, growing, loving, and the legacy it imprints on this world—it is a matter of obedience to your purpose and mission of your marriage.

Jehovah-Jireh & Jehovah-El Elohim

In many regards, the discussion in the Bible about provision is almost irrelevant in today's economy. Much of the gender specifics purported by the Bible do not even appear applicable when considering the advancement and contributions of women in our current society as it relates to financial provision. I will discuss this in greater detail in the upcoming chapters. One thing, however, is consistent: God is your Jehovah-Jireh (Genesis 22:14 & Numbers 20:7-11), which means provider, and Jehovah-El Elohim (Genesis 17:7; Jeremiah 31:33), which means creator, might, and strength, through whom we are protected. You are not the provider and protector of your family. I am not saying that you are not or should not be gainfully employed. I am not saying you should not defend yourself or your loved ones. But let us use these two terms separately and not interchangeably: gainfully employed versus provider. Men and women, as their lives necessitate, ought to be gainfully employed. On the other hand, God is our provider.

What if God told you to leave your job and start a business or go into full-time ministry? We tend to link the male identity to provision, and provision tends to mostly be defined as financial. So are you now less of a man if you are not working? Some would argue that God would not tell you to stop working because it may place the financial burden on your wife. But if she was not working, would the financial burden not be on you? Is she not qualified to be gainfully employed? No matter how you want to splice the topic, neither your job or your wife's job are a means of provision. If she died, to whom would you look for provision? If you died, to whom would she look? We can tear down the walls of conflict by focusing on the meta-values of spiritual matters as it relates to provision. God is our provider.

If husband and wife can come to understand that God provides for them through their job and other means, then the income difference will make no difference because it all comes from God. Psalms 24 makes the matter clear, "The earth is the Lord's, and the fullness thereof; the world, and they that dwell therein." Psalms 50:10 says, "For every beast of the forest *is* mine, *and* the cattle upon a thousand hills." Unfortunately, some people have to lose in order to be reminded who the real provider is. The contentious cycle between men and women and their roles can easily be avoided by acknowledging the true provider over their lives is Jehovah, Allah, Akuj, or the name by which you call God.

Furthermore, financial provision is only one aspect of being a provider. The role of provider more robustly includes spiritual, emotional, and physical support, bringing us back to the topic of leadership. Effective leadership is a spiritual undertaking and, in the process, provides support, encouragement, and a family vision for their spouse. Providers help fold clothes, wash dishes, vacuum, dust, sweep, mop, fix the j-trap, install appliances, clear the gutter, help the children with homework, encourage their wives, crack jokes, pray for and with the family, be life-long learners, and keep the environment light-hearted. Provision comes in so many ways. Sometimes you will need to provide your wife a hug or a thank you. Sometimes you will provide her a romantic setting to pamper her. Sometimes you will provide her a sit-down conversation about an issue she needs to address. Sometimes you will provide her a nice pat on the butt just to let her know you still find her sexy. The above stated are much more akin to provision because they demonstrate an altruistic lifestyle that goes way beyond being gainfully employed.

Protector

In like manner to provision, God is also the protector of your family. Psalms 18 recognizes God as the power to call upon for safety and refuge. This does not mean you move your family into a crime-ridden neighborhood and take the front door off the hinge under the guise that God is your protector. That is not wisdom. Effective leadership employs and deploys with wisdom. Protection is also an emotional, spiritual, and physical undertaking. From a physical standpoint, let us be realistic about it. Where are you when your child leaves your home to walk to school and your wife drives to work? Do you fly above your daughter ready to stand between her and a car that jumps the curb? Or do you hang in the shadows ready to unhand the thief ready to snatch your wife's purse? Every time your wife and children leave your presence it is nothing but the mercy of God that returns them home safely. Even in the home there are dangers at every turn. On numerous occasions I have had to thank God for showing mercy to my children who almost smashed their fingers, ran into the sliding glass door, slipped on spilled water, or nearly missed running their head into a pointy object. God is your protector and protects them through you and absent you. God also protects us from emotional and spiritual harm through the counsel and watchfulness of our wives as we also do the same for them. Provision and protection both belong to God.

Relationship with God (Love the Lord Thy God)

The inescapable truth is that the most important relationship you will ever have is the one you have with yourself and God. And your ultimate goal is to grow in that relationship and allow it to manifest in how you manage your emotions and present your bodies as a living sacrifice (Romans 12:1).

Moreover, in all that you do, there is one charge given to all men and women, whether single or married: "Love the Lord thy God with all thy heart, and with all thy soul, and with all thy strength, and with all thy mind; and thy neighbor as thyself" (Luke 10:27). (Your wife is also your neighbor; you are her neighbor as well—she should love you.) You can splice the topic of finances, domestic duties, family duties, childrearing, sex, communication, and many more topics that orbits marriages, but the successful planning, managing, and implementing of any strategy will always reflect the personal relationship that every man and woman is required to have with God.

The characters of the Bible, from Adam in Genesis to John in Revelations, were each engaged in a one-on-one relationship with God. One-on-one equals one. Romans 14:11 states, "For it is written, as I live, saith the Lord, every knee shall bow to me, and every tongue shall confess to God." This passage of Scripture is not gender specific. Verses 12-13 reads, "So then every one of us shall give account of himself to God. Let us not therefore judge one another anymore: but judge this rather, that no man put a stumbling block or an occasion to fall in his brother's way." The words "himself" or "brother" does not confine the principled Scripture to men only. The woman is simply a man with a womb, so a man nevertheless.

Our spirituality is the relationship we have with self and God. Our relationship with self and God is then reflected and transferred into our relationship with others, including our spouse. The relationship building process with self, God, and spouse is incumbent on both parties. Another person cannot be more responsible for your spiritual growth than you. I have observed a level of confusion in Christian churches that seems to create a paradox for women by moving them away from their own sense of spirituality to the spiritual guidance offered by their husband. In so doing, women place the burden of their spiritual growth onto their husbands because the husband, viewed as leader and head of the household, is also viewed as the spiritual leader of the house. This breathes a level of unaccountability in her and places an overbearing responsibility on the husband. We are each responsible for our spiritual growth.

On the other hand, many men shun the idea of her spirituality because the patriarchal religious narrative has promoted him as the conduit between God and wife. Men and women support this idea with the Scripture 1 Corinthians 11:3 which states the man is the head of the woman and Christ is the head of man. However, the best a wife can offer her husband or a husband can offer his wife is reflective of the relationship she or he, of their own free will, has with God.

CIRCLE

a poem

"I love the Lord because He first loved me"
is how the song goes.
of course, He loved me first;
He knew me before the foundation of the earth
He loved me when time –
well, when there was no such thing.
He loved me before an atom and nucleus
knew to be lovers.
He loved me before love had any other
definition;
when love was defined as love.
I love Him too.
though He loving me first is half the view.
we rationalize and contextualize,
in other words, humanize,
in the process humiliate and falsify
what humans say symbolize love
but love, all four letters,
as simple and powerful as God himself,
can only be actualized as His Christ,
once crucified in order to purify,
for God so loved the world that He gave
His only begotten sun
to the dark side of the moon and
while he returned soon, nevertheless
God loved us so much that He
sacrificed His love.

I love the Lord because He first loved me,
for loving me was a part of He
that in the creation of me,
was created love returned,
called love and loyalty.
I love Him because the choice
has been made easy to see,
to love Him is to love me.
before the foundation of the earth
He outlined my destiny,
and I quote, "to rest in me"
for to be one with He is to be
the son that He loved first,
loved unselfishly,
for He gave His only begotten son
for all of we to become one
with He and love Him because
He first loved me.

STRAIGHTENING THE NARRATIVE OF ADAM & EVE

CHAPTER 5

"You're a failure. I thought I would have been further along in life with someone like you," she said as she stared down at me, again, sitting on the same edge of that couch where I cried nearly eight years earlier pleading for her to give me her attention. Her words resonated to my core. At this moment, I was out of work, because of my own negligence, trying to find myself and find a job. Interestingly enough, it was during this time of not working when some crucial statements from my wife at the time were directed toward me. I had never been called a failure before. I was student body president at my undergraduate university, director of my department early in my professional career, and had achieved numerous other successes as a young adult—yet, here I am being called a failure.

As I searched for a job and started to run my own business in the meantime, she told me, "I didn't marry a man to take care of him." I was speechless and numb, to say the least. I was employed for nearly eight years out of our nine-year marriage. During those eight years my wife at the time had been terminated from two jobs and bounced between three more jobs. I had always worked, managed the finances, and gone above and beyond my share of managing the home. In fact, my wife at the time had been through five years of schooling for her bachelor's and master's degree while I worked full-time, did most of the rearing pertaining to our children, and completed most of the household chores. But somehow, now unemployed for ten months, I was considered a non-progressive failure and freeloader.

I fell into a deep depression while trying to figure out who I was and what I was worth. I had never felt good enough for her, right enough for her. Now a name to my unworthiness had been identified: failure. It echoed around me. The public face of trying to keep it together began to crack like medieval statues that could no longer resist the persistence of rain and sun. But it was these experiences that brought great insight. And like King Solomon, great insight came about my duty as a man.

IT'S NOT YOUR JOB TO PROVIDE & PROTECT

The male identity, the construct of norms, social meanings, and institutional identity, is mostly shaped by the acceptance of the social contract that the function of a man is "provider and protector" of women and families. However, it is NOT the categorial function of a man to provide and protect. Overwhelmingly, men have been diluted to just those two basic qualities. As mentioned before, God is our provider and protector. A man cannot provide and protect unless he too is provided for and protected. As God is the provider and protector, men then, are stewards of the resources we have been provided. You cannot live your life with one foot believing God is your Jehovah-Jireh & Jehovah-El Elohim, and the other foot also believing that you are your own Jehovah-Jireh & Jehovah-El Elohim.

As a steward, you are responsible for managing, supervising, or tending to the resources provided by God. As such, being gainfully employed is advisable. You should also understand the role you assume for the physical, emotional, and spiritual welfare of your family. You assume this role by being a proper steward of the resources you have been provided. The important reason for this distinction is that you assume your role as husband with the understanding that your identity is not enveloped in your ability to provide and protect. It is enveloped within your ability to walk in your purpose and be a good steward. Being defined by your purpose is far different from being defined by your ability to provide and protect. In fact, the entire enterprise of provision and protection is steeped in patriarchy, hegemony, and misguided principles of masculinity and femininity.

ADAM & EVE

The role of a man as provider and protector is also largely substantiated through religious indoctrination starting with the story of Adam and Eve. It is often taught that the first thing God did after creating Adam was to give him a job. Therefore, it is expected that a man should work. After all, Adam was working. Let's break this down. So, you mean to tell me that in all of God's glory, He needed to create a man in order to give names to plants and animals? How did Adam even know to call a cow a "cow" or a beetle a "beetle?" How much was Adam paid? Was he on salary or an hourly wage? Was he working for food and shelter? Was he a part of a group health insurance plan? Did he have a 401K? How many years of work before being vested? The problem is that we conflate spiritual things with natural things and attempt to apply it to a physical world with man-made concepts. The story of Adam and Eve is NOT about gender roles.

The story of Adam and Eve is a multi-layered spiritual metaphor outlining the relationship we all have with God and the double consciousness we each experience in our attempt to overcome evil and do what is good and proper. It is a battle each person undertakes. Some people fare better than others in this internal fight, but it is innate to the human process. Note the duality of the Garden of Eden: man and woman; tree of life versus the tree of knowledge of good and evil; and the word of God versus the words of the serpent. These are symbols, not necessarily actual entities.

God created both Adam and Eve when he created Adam. God later put Adam in a deep sleep and took out his rib, from which Eve was formed. (When was the last time your woman was taken from your actual rib?) Adam, the man, contained within him a susceptible part of himself, the woman, called Eve. This is not the actual man or the actual woman, but characters symbolic of our higher consciousness (Adam/man) and our lower consciousness (Eve/woman). God tells our higher consciousness (greater selves) to choose life and walk in his commandments in the presence of God. However, our lower consciousness (lesser self) is susceptible to the deception of the world, the flesh, and the devil, summarily presented as the serpent. In unwatchfulness, people allow their greater self to be deceived by their lower self, therefore falling out of grace with God and in need of redemption.

God did not give Adam a job (to provide and protect). What would Adam have provided to Eve that was not already provided in the Garden? Please do not fly past that question. Again, I ask: what would Adam have provided to Eve that was not already provided in the Garden created by God? In other words, God was the provider. Adam simply needed to be obedient to God's word to dress and keep the Garden, which is also to say, be a good steward. As for protection, God gave Adam the means of which to protect Eve by eating from the tree of life. Again, obedience and good steward was at the core of Adam's responsibility toward mentoring his lower self to the understanding of his higher self. Viewing the story of Adam and Eve as an outline on gender roles is murky, inconsistent, and an illogical attempt to apply spiritual matters to a physical, material world.

God gave Adam purpose and authority over all things in the Garden—a sphere of influence that God had delineated for Adam to inhabit. Have you ever allowed a friend, or family member, business partner, or stranger to deter you from the word, mandate, or vision that you were certain was God-given? If so, then in that moment, they were a deceived Eve who had brought to you an ill-advised word for which you became susceptible. It resulted in a breakage from the purpose God had assigned to you. You moved from eating of the tree of life to believing a lie from a deceived individual who assured you that you would not die, when in fact, you did die. The vision died when it was moved from outside of the Garden, the perfect will of God. Now, you have to till the ground, working harder than you had to before, until you are redeemed back into the favor of God.

The story of Adam and Eve does not tell men and women how to behave as a couple other than stating that man and wife shall be one flesh. And in saying so, we still observe the duality of Adam and Eve and their unification in purpose as one joint entity. Furthermore, Eve was Adam's helpmeet, but the Scripture shows we are helpers one to another (1 Thessalonians 5:11). Your business partner, best friend, and even your children are your helpmeet. How rudimentary of us, as humans, to operationalize the story of Adam and Eve for our human purpose—because it is used to support a hierarchical structure that gives men power over women.

THE PUNISHMENTS FOR ADAM AND EVE (GENESIS 3:15-19)

Genesis 3:15-19 paints a demoralizing end to Adam and Eve's residence in the Garden of Eden. Where they once interacted with God in the Garden, they now found themselves separated from His presence because of their disobedience. The serpent said they would not surely die, but little did Eve know at the time death meant separation from God, a spiritual death. In separation, God doled out the following punishment to Adam and Eve:

Woman (Eve)

- *Greatly multiply thy sorrow and thy conception*
- *In sorrow thou shalt bring forth children*
- *Desire shall be to thy husband,*
- *Husband shall rule over thee*

Man (Adam)

- *Cursed is the ground for thy sake*
- *In sorrow shalt thou eat of the ground all the days of thy life*

- *Thorns and thistles shall the ground bring forth to thee*
- *Eat the herb of the field*
- *In the sweat of thy face shalt thou eat bread*

In short, a man's rule over women is her punishment. In this very verse (Genesis 3:16) was the establishment of patriarchy, hegemony, and hypermasculinity wherein women are emotionally, spiritually, and physically subjugated to male authority and headship. We have historically observed this occur to their detriment, including economically, politically, religiously, socially, and psychologically. As it is clearly written in Scripture, his leadership and her desire toward his leadership is part of the damned nature of women.

Additionally, the man's act of provision is also his punishment. There was nothing for Adam to provide to Eve that was not already provided by God in the Garden of Eden. The only thing left for Adam to provide Eve was leadership—leading her to remain in the obedience of God. Our higher consciousness is responsible for building up our lower consciousness to not be greater than, but as our higher consciousness. However, God's punishment to Adam lowered his "eating" to the ground, which was now polluted with thorns and thistles. In other words, the sustenance of God through the Garden of Eden was now replaced with hardship and labor. In this state, both men and women experience sorrow.

The redemptive work of Jesus Christ's death, burial, resurrection, and ascension as the coming of the second Adam (1 Corinthians 15:45-48) corrected the fallen state of mankind. We are no longer subjected to the cursed and sinful nature of the human condition; we have a pathway back to the Garden of Eden through Christ Jesus. As such, if Adam and Eve were punished, Christ, the sacrificial lamb (John 1:29) removed the punishment. Yet, people often confuse the punishment imparted to Adam and Eve for their disobedience as appropriate beliefs about men and women and the romantic, marital space they share. We now have an opportunity to "put forth our hand, and take also of the tree of life, and eat, and live forever" (Genesis 3:22), which no longer subjects women to the sorrow of childbirth and male hegemony, and men to the hardships of provision. By returning to the Garden of Eden, you return to a state of stewardship, because there was nothing that Adam or Eve had to provide to each other that was not already provided by God.

RELIGION AND THE SOCIAL CONSTRUCT

Religion may be the most influential tactic in impacting the social, political, psychological, and economic worlds in which we live. But these systems of beliefs are built on top of one another, specifically beginning with the matter of provision. The dominating belief that it is a man's responsibility to provide for and protect his wife immediately minimizes the woman's role and subjugates her to the dominance of men. Women have bought into this concept of provision and protection because it makes her the object of the man's responsibility, which means she is socially declared less responsible for herself and less accountable for the relationship. In return for provision and protection, the woman pledges her body to fulfill his sexual desire for procreation and recreation. The social quid quo pro reinforces the belief that, unlike women, men are sexual beings who go to major extents for sexual conquests.

For centuries, major world religions throughout many countries have pushed a patriarchal agenda. These beliefs often begin in the church, supported by Scripture that says the man is the head of the woman (1 Corinthians 11:3). Women, in their search for a husband, are hoping to find a man who provides **headship to their**

liking. The buy-in of male headship builds from the church into our moral and social beliefs, then to our ways of forming organizations, corporations and legislation, and finally into a full-blown case of "let's-think-for-women-because-they-can't-think-for-themselves," a mentality held by both men and women. By the time the beliefs surrounding gender roles leave the church and enter the larger society, you find practices and legislation that exert power and control over women—ironically, created by men, absent the input of women, yet supported by women who pass along these teachings and practices to younger girls. Interestingly enough, this same paradigm supports the wrongdoing of men, allowing "men to be men," while the same unjust men exercise discipline over women for her "wrongdoing."

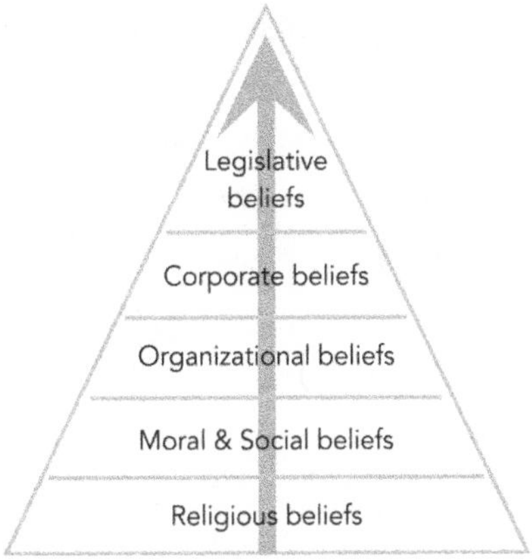

Accordingly, religious ideologies are often the underpinnings as to why women cannot participate in certain activities throughout societies, such as driving, playing sports, voting, and holding certain high-level positions in business or government. The social contract of provision and protection is also the antecedent to the conflict, domination, and hierarchy of power that has been abused by men for centuries. It has, in fact, created an identity crisis within men in an ever-increasing world centered on the control of resources, of which women have historically been viewed as a resource or property. Men are trapped in an ongoing attempt to demonstrate their masculinity in an attempt to affirm their manhood. Part of that masculinity is demonstrated through domination over women. Women, in this framework, are bought and contractually owned through marriage.

Additionally, because provision and protection, as a starting point, relinquishes power and control over to the man, it furthers the belief that **Christ polices the man as the man polices the woman**. Let's explore the hierarchy of God, Christ, man, then woman discussed in 1 Corinthians 11. The construct is as follows: God, a deity and an entity that is not human, is deemed the head of the (human) man; meanwhile, a (human) man is the head of the (human) woman. In other words, the invisible God is over the man, while the visible and very human man is over the woman. A woman is thereby subjected to the human shortcomings of a man, while the man is only governed by a deity that is not subjected to the shortcomings of humanity. How convenient for men and oppressive for women—an unbalanced level of responsibility for men, and an unfortunate situation for women. The interpretation of this hierarchy has been traditionally mischaracterized by the church, providing an unbalanced system of checks and balances and a loophole to patriarchy and male hegemony. Unfortunately, many women have also bought into the idea of being the weaker, lesser, subordinate sex as taught to them through religion and socialization for the promise of false conveniences sold as provision and protection.

POWER DYNAMICS

To believe that another person is responsible for your provision and protection automatically renders power and control over to the individual identified as the responsible party. Therefore, to place the male figure as provider places him at the center of power and control in the relationship. This aligns well with the power and authority established through headship. In this design, the best a woman can hope for is a benevolent dictator; otherwise, power is easily abused. Women have embraced the structure of provision and protection because, as mentioned before, it is convenient. But it comes at the cost of them being treated as the lesser sex. However, women are not unintentional creatures. Like any human being, women pursue and exploit power in other ways. Women have found equal power in their pseudo-subordinate roles. As mentioned before, women are not second to men. Nonetheless, the foundation of these beliefs surrounding provision and protection help to prop up hyper-masculinity and male dominance over a woman's access to upward mobility, lifestyle, and her own body (the body he ultimately provides for, therefore, owns). The social quid pro quo of provision and protection is an exchange for sexual procreation and recreation, supporting a prostitution-styled mindset. After all, we are a transactional society. The power and control bequest to men through provision and protection creates the following outcomes:

- Women are socialized to see themselves as less responsible and accountable for themselves;
- Women might see themselves at the center of relationships as the one to be cared for (centerfolding);

- Women may use their body as a bargaining chip in exchange for goods and services;
- Women are not considered sexual beings, yet taught their sexuality is one of their greatest assets—the very thing that is also often taken advantage of;
- Men are viewed as solely responsible for financial provision, thereby making his income his greatest asset;
- Men are advertised as sexually-motivated beings;
- Men are willing to exchange provision and protection for sex.

The construct of provision and protection runs you right into a slippery slope that overruns your true identity as a man. Many men discover they are really not the "head" of anything in a marriage, especially when the expectation to provide is based on the evaluation and expectation of the woman. This is how she derives power. The effects of coming up short in the area of provision have left many men discouraged, emasculated, said to not be a "real man," divorced, and mocked as failures. Her ability to define the man's identity based on his ability to provide is a serious power often exercised by women. It also gives her power over how he is perceived by others within the community. Women are not second to men, nor are they emotionally or spiritually weaker. And where women may usually be physically weaker than a man, it is not to misinterpret "weaker" for being weak.

As seen through the story of Adam and Eve, the male figure in the Bible is often the symbol of headship, power, or the representative of the Holy Spirit. The female figure is often the symbol of susceptibility to evil, deception, or the representative of the Soul. But let's quickly note that Adam (man) became susceptible to wrongdoing, albeit presented through Eve, he was susceptible nonetheless

(Genesis 3:6). God and Christ are presented in male form to symbolize headship and power, but God is neither male or female. The Bible makes it clear that God and Christ, His son, are Spirit (John 4:24). The Bible further makes it clear that gender is a non-factor in Heavenly places. The Book of Galatians 3:28 says "There is neither Jew nor Greek, there is neither bond nor free, there is neither male nor female: for ye are all one in Christ Jesus." Apostle Paul's hierarchical structure delineated in Ephesians 5:21-33, which states Christ is the head of the husband, who is the head of the wife, builds up to verse 32, which states, "This is a great mystery: but I speak concerning Christ and the church." Again, we see symbolism throughout the Bible, which posits mankind as the bride of Christ.

Accordingly, the real submission of husband and wife is mankind (wife) to Christ (husband). This means the human being, male and female, constitute mankind. A man, the male gender, by definition is not superior to a woman. The buy-in to man as provider and protector is misleading and a disproportionate allocation of power. Provision and protection are a slippery slope that amounts to ownership. Our gender-related powers are distributed differently and contribute in different ways. However, different does not make any gender lesser or greater.

THE DUTY OF A MAN

CHAPTER 6

It is a man's duty to lead, not provide. The job of provision and protection, as mentioned in Chapter 4, belongs to God. As a matter of fact, contrary to popular belief and in spite of how many times you will hear people say it, the Bible does not say it is a man's job to provide. Provision as the duty of a man is NOT biblically supported. You have been tricked, my friend, bamboozled, and hoodwinked, especially as it relates to provision as a financial obligation. The social conversation has unfortunately and increasingly placed less focus on the emotional and spiritual need for provision and protection, and misappropriate Scripture for physical and financial matters. You have been given a larger and unfair share of the responsibility.

Again, provision and protection are God's job. Your job is to build a relationship with God and be a good steward over what has been given within your purview of responsibilities, and throughout that process, lead. But it is not a Scripturally-based declaration, nor is it the categorical function of a man to work and be the financier of the family. However, you will hear this statement made over and over again and said to be Scripturally supported—it is not. The consistent hammering of that assertion puts the carriage in front of the horse. I insist, **provision and protection are found within leadership**. The mantra that it is a man's responsibility to provide and protect corners men into an unbalanced role. The effects of cornering the man's categorical function as provider are several:

- Dilutes the man's categorial function to a paycheck, often assigning the quality of his manhood to his income;
- Dismisses or overlooks the role of a woman to also provide for and protect her husband;
- Fails to acknowledge the need of the man to feel spiritually, emotionally, and physically safe as the notion of protection is often discussed as a unidirectional responsibility toward women and children;
- Creates a different expectation for the man in the marriage that results in him usually being economically, religiously, and socially more accountable for the success of the relationship;
- The metric of the relationship success is largely based on his doing, not hers;
- Subjugates the woman because the role of provider and protector is inherently a position of power, invariably hierarchical, and thereby authoritative of the entity that falls under the purview of provision and protection.

Also important to note is that the mantra of man as provider is **not** Scripturally based. The Bible says to:

- Live in understanding with her (1 Peter 3:7)
- Honor her as the weaker vessel (1 Peter 3:7)
- Love her (Colossians 3:19)
- Love her as your own body (Ephesians 5:28)
- Do not be harsh with her (Colossians 3:19)
- Cleave to her (Genesis 2:24)
- Give her due benevolence (1 Corinthians 7:4)
- Submit one to another (Ephesians 5:21)
- Be kind, tenderhearted, forgiving one another (Ephesians 4:32)

The interpretation and practice of Scripture is the seed to much conflict, discontent and misguided expectations of men regarding finance and marriage in general. With most of the Bible written in a **male centric voice**, the "burden of provision" has inadvertently been placed onto the man. The challenge in Scripture is that the men who wrote much of the text did so in a masculine-centered form by using "he, him, or man." This occurred mainly because the books of the Bible were mostly written by men to a male-reading audience. However, text written in masculine form also serves as instructive to the general public, women included. In response to the heavy male centered voice, in the 21ST century, the reference to gender in manuals and guides have been updated to remove "he" or "him" to reflect "his and her" or "she." Why? Because people recognized the overabundance of the masculine-centered voice to the exclusion of women. To say the least, much of the text in the Bible is apropos to both male and female genders. Obvious by now, the male centric voice throughout the Bible has greatly shaped biblical exegesis to be defined as speaking of the male gender, when in fact it speaks to mankind (all human beings). For example:

1 Corinthians 13:11

> "When I was a child, I spake as a child, I understood as a child, I thought as a child: but when I became a man, I put away childish things."

The Scripture's use of the word "man" does not confine the meaning, interpretation, or integrity to be the requirement of the male gender only. The universal truth of the Scripture is that individuals must transition from childhood to adulthood, from immaturity to maturity, and from the foolish to the wise. In no shape or form does 1 Corinthians 13:11 mean that only males put away childish things as they move into manhood; which is to say, women do not put away childish things as they move into womanhood. Similarly, the declaration that a man who does not provide for his house is worse than an infidel contains the universal truth that family is supposed to take care of family—not that males only are supposed to take care of family. We see another mixture of the masculine-centered voice in Ephesians 6:1-4.

Ephesians 6:1-4

> "Children, obey your parents in the Lord: for this is right. Honour thy father and mother (which is the first commandment with promise); That it may be well with thee, and thou mayest live long on the earth. And, ye fathers, provoke not your children to wrath: but bring them up in the nurture and admonition of the Lord."

After the Scripture opens up about obedience and honor to both father and mother, the fourth verse says "ye fathers, provoke not your children to wrath." The Scripture no longer includes mothers. Does this mean mothers do not provoke their children to wrath? Does this also mean only fathers can "nurture and admonish" the children? What made the writer switch from "father and mother" to just father? Maybe the writer was considering a father-to-son relationship and overlooked a mother-to-daughter relationship. Maybe the writer thought fathers tended to deal more harshly with children. Whatever the case, it is inconsequential. The intent of the writer is clear. You and I know that, albeit "mothers" is no longer mentioned, mothers are capable of provoking their children, something from which they should refrain. In fact, provocation is a biblical precept that is advised against. Moreover, mothers share in the responsibility of nurturing and admonishing their children.

1 Timothy 5:8

> "But if any provide not for his own, and especially for those of his own house, he hath denied the faith, and is worse than an infidel."

We can only understand this one verse by first understanding the context of the entire chapter. The chapter is first and foremost about household support, not male provision. Verse 1-16 is a soliloquy on how the church and family members should be caretakers of the widows of their family. It is incorrect to think the conversation on widows included a mandate for males only to follow.

Second, pay attention to the word "house" in the Scripture. "House" during these times (as it still does today) meant the integrity of the family/last name, inclusive of aunts, uncles, grandmothers, nephews, nieces, cousins, and other relatives. Marriages were often performed as strategic moves to create alliances amongst *houses.*

Some revisions of the Bible have reinterpreted the Scripture of "his own house" to say 'relatives' and more directly 'his own family'—but that is semantics. Summarily, the Scripture is a point of order written in generic form for family members to take care of family. The "his own house" of verse 8 is written in masculine form. But is it not also her house?

2 Thessalonians 3:10

> "For even when we were with you, this we commanded you, that if any would not work, neither should he eat."

Again, we can only understand this one verse by first understanding the context of the entire chapter. Bearing that in mind, most of Chapter 3 was written to men and "brethren" focused on correcting disorderly conduct and the need to sever relationships with people they knew to be disorderly.

Apostle Paul's admonishment of 'working to eat' aligns with the sense of order he was trying to establish. Apostle Paul, writing in a masculine-centered voice, was not speaking in general to men, but specifically to the group of men with whom he walked. Throughout the New Testament you will find no other major female characters than Mary, Joseph's wife, and Mary Magdalene. Considering that fact, Apostle Paul, as seen, would have almost always spoken in masculine form as on most occasions (if not all) his letters were written to other men.

Most importantly, verse 11 explains the need for Apostle Paul's admonishment given in verse 10. Verse 11 states some of the men "walk among them disorderly, working not at all, but busybodies." In other words, some of the men do very little or nothing throughout the day but are front and center when food is served. Apostle Paul's admonition sounded more like a discussion on organizational culture than on gender roles. Have you ever observed an unproductive staff member eat lunch alongside the staff members who have worked diligently? In fact, for those unproductive members, the most productive part of their day was their high motivation to eat.

I agree that we can pull a global lesson from Apostle Paul's admonishment. People should be productive, contributing members of society, people should not be lazy and then expect to "eat" similarly to those who were diligent. Productive people should separate themselves from unproductive individuals. But again, NOTHING within this Scripture says this is the requirement of men only. The meta-value of the Scripture is clearly apropos to both men and women.

1 Peter 3:7

> "Likewise, ye husbands, dwell with them according to knowledge, giving honour unto the wife, as unto the weaker vessel, and as being heirs together of the grace of life; that your prayers be not hindered."

The entire 1 Peter, Chapter 3 is a beautiful admonishment for living together as husband and wife. Verse 7 however, is often twisted by readers to garner power for domination in a relationship, shifting the focus from the other delights offered throughout the chapter. Verse 7 is foundational in presenting women as weaker than a man, often the justification for abuse against women or the manipulative practices of women against men. The first inclination of the word "weaker" is usually toward her physical strength. It is substantiated that men typically have more upper-body strength than the typical woman. However, all men are not physically stronger than all women. As mentioned before, where women may usually be physically weaker than a man, we should not misinterpret "weaker" for weak.

Viewed as power, physical strength is the ability to exert force for a short period of time. However, women display a type of strength through endurance. Exerting force versus endurance is the difference between the sprinter and the long-distance runner. Each runner is respected and revered for their ability in their respective area. In fact, strength and endurance training is a well-rounded and necessary workout. Her endurance is best exemplified through her child-bearing process—something a man cannot do.

The second inclination is regarding her emotions. To see her as emotionally weaker falsely props up the belief that men are more logical thinkers, a more desirable trait for leadership. As such, we muffle the emotionality of young boys because men are not supposed to emote. The truth is, men are equally emotional, and emotions will come out one way or the other, sooner or later in some shape or form. The quelled emotions of men often turn into poor emotional management, resentment, and hyper-masculinity. Most wars started throughout the entire history of the world were started by an emotional man.

Unfortunately, the notion of "weaker vessel" has also spilled over into other areas to include 1) the belief that the woman ought to be financially weaker, thereby needing a man to provide for her; 2) morally weaker, an ode to the susceptibility of Eve in the Garden of Eden; and 3) intellectually weaker, due to her emotional state. Do you see the chasm that leads toward intimidation, domination, and manipulation through centuries of patriarchal leadership? On the other hand, women, knowing they are not "weaker" by any of these measures, yet perceived as such, notoriously use the appearance of weakness to their advantage by playing possum.

Note that even in being referred to as the "weaker vessel," there is still a call to honour one's wife because she is also a joint-heir of Christ (Romans 8:17). On the strength of you and your wife being joint-heirs, I vigorously contend that she is NOT the weaker vessel. 2 Timothy 1:7 says we have been given power, love, and a sound mind. Philippians 4:13 says we can do all things through Christ who strengthens us.

1 Timothy 3:4-5

> "One that ruleth well his own house, having his children in subjection with all gravity; (For if a man know not how to rule his own house, how shall he take care of the church of God?)"

1 Timothy, Chapter 3 contextually addresses the moral prerequisite for a man desiring the office of bishop. The word "ruleth" simply means to lead. The Scripture more precisely says "ruleth well," focusing on the importance of proper leadership. Of certainty, the leader of God's people must also lead within the home. While this Scripture is not an instance of a masculine-centered voice, it focuses on a male becoming bishop. The expressed standards were not to the exclusion of women as leaders within the home or to assert the man's leadership over the wife. The principles of 1 Timothy, Chapter 3 speaks to order, leadership, and management.

Also, Verse 3 says the bishop should lead "having his children in subjection with all gravity." The only mention of wife in 1 Timothy, Chapter 3 is that bishops and deacons have only one. If you contend that the wife is also part of the house, then why did the Scripture not mention having the wife under subjection? It is inconsequential because the focus of the chapter is about becoming a bishop, not gender roles or an exposé on female subjugation.

1 Timothy 2:9-15

> "In like manner also, that women adorn themselves in modest apparel, with shamefacedness and sobriety; not with braided hair, or gold, or pearls, or costly array; But (which becometh women professing godliness) with good works. Let the woman learn in silence with all subjection. But I suffer not a woman to teach, nor to usurp authority over the man, but to be in silence. For Adam was first formed, then Eve. And Adam was not deceived, but the woman being deceived was in the transgression. Notwithstanding she shall be saved in childbearing, if they continue in faith and charity and holiness with sobriety."

Again, this Scripture is used to dominate women: be seen and not heard; unpermitted, and thereby incapable of leading; second to a man; required to be mild-mannered; and she is more easily susceptible to deception due to her emotions. Let's say this was the case. Would she not know better by now? After all, it has been two thousand years since this text was written. Do children not grow up to be responsible adults? Can the woman not evolve?

What is the woman to do with her knowledge after she has learned in subjection or is she to be perpetually a learner in her subjection? However, Jesus spoke in Mathews 10:24 saying, "It is enough for the disciple that he be as his master, and the servant as his lord..." John 15:15 shows a pathway from servitude to friendship. If I were a woman, I would be confused by these varying Scriptures. Which is it? Is she forever less than a man or "I can do all things through Christ which strengtheneth me" (Philippians 4:13)? Or was that Scripture reserved for men only?

The natural propensity of any human being is to find a pathway from domination. Children rebel against parents in an effort to express independence and individuality. Why would the knowledgeable women, in subjection, taught by men for centuries, at some point or another not want to demonstrate her autonomy and individuality? The human spirit demands it of any human being.

In Verse 14, referring to Eve as deceived, does this mean a man cannot be deceived? Or does it mean only a woman can bring deception to a man as Eve brought it to Adam? John 10:10 says "The thief cometh not, but for to steal, and to kill, and to destroy." It doesn't say the woman cometh. According to the story of Samson in the Book of Judges, he was told not to marry a certain type of woman. Therefore, was Samson deceived or simply disobedient in his pursuit of Delilah? Answer: he was disobedient, not deceived. What woman deceived Jonah from going to Nineveh? What woman deceived Moses when he struck the rock a second time instead of following God's instructions to speak to the rock? Women are not the cause of men's fate. One's gender does not make them more vulnerable to the ills of spiritual depravity.

Men and women have bought into these ideals that subjugate and victimize both men and women because, at no level, do these beliefs, practices, and legislation take into consideration the ability, experience, or character of the man or woman. Handing out positions at a company before interviewing and assessing skill level is ill advised. Yet society hands out gender roles that eventually emasculate men and women as men are forced into a role above their head while women are forced into a role belittling their worth. I call this belief of men as provider and protector the Superhero Fallacy. Men and women have been sold on the man as the superhero and the woman as the damsel in distress. In other words, women need saving and men are the savior. Believing you are the superhero may lead to one of two extremes: 1) an inflated sense of self, which leads to hyper-masculinity, or 2) an overwhelming sense of responsibility, which boils you down to a paycheck and a tool. A woman's buy-in to being the *damsel in distress* leads her to be more reliant on a man and demotes accountability of herself. It also exposes her vulnerabilities, which in effect, promotes a victim mentality. Women are just as heroic as men in contributing to the betterment of one another.

Additionally, many women tend to like the convenience that comes with the idea that a man is ultimately responsible for providing and protecting. But the following conundrum occurs. The challenge with women who want equality in access, education, and upward mobility in the 21ST century is that they simultaneously do not want equality in responsibility for provision and protection. Many of them want to exercise the convenience of receiving both privileges. Euro-centric individualism has made gynocentric behaviors an entitlement to women. However, over time we find that these gender roles are destructive to both men and women as they promote the punishing practices that accompanied man's removal from the Garden of Eden. My discourse throughout this chapter distills into the following summative analysis which I refer to as the Provision-to-Power Theory.

PROVISION TO POWER THEORY

The Provision-to-Power Theory deduces men endure a fractured social identity caused by an overbearing focus placed on being the financial provider. Men as the sole or the larger responsible party for financial provision has been a widely held view across many societies for centuries.

- First, the emphasis on the role of financial provision promotes a power imbalance that segues men into 1) an attitude of dominance and control and 2) an inferior view of women. These pervasive thoughts become masked as the definition of manhood. The religious underpinnings of provision (and protection) has substantiated and codified these ideals into normal society. These concepts deeply impact the psyche and attitudes of men into ways of thinking that lead them away from their purpose of leadership into a mode of survival and a confused state of self-actualization.
- Second and more specifically, the Bible does not contextually state it is the responsibility of a man to provide, nor does it systematically sustain the belief that the man is the head of the woman. Contextual evidence of popular Scriptures used to support these claims proves that a reading of the chapter in its entirety paints a different picture than isolated verses.
- Third, women who subscribe to this social norm of male provision do so in anticipation of being relieved from the financial responsibility and accountability of the relationship. In spite of her ability as an able-bodied, emotionally mature adult with effective communica-

tion, management, and problem-solving skills, he is still accountable to do the necessary to maintain his family unit. Women also tend to be substantially more vocal about upholding the institution of men as the financially responsible party for the relationship, making financials one of the most central aspects of romantic relationships.

- Fourth, women who subscribe to this belief see the design as advantageous, and thereby, succumb to a socially approved victim mentality in which they perpetuate an inferior status as the weaker sex. However, they simultaneously cite other intangible qualities as their strength to extinguish the narrative of women as weaker. In other words, they play coy as the "weaker" sex and simultaneously invoke their strength to balance the playing field.
- Fifth, women do not see themselves as less capable than a man, but in full soundness of mind, see the man as responsible for their well-being. Women use the very social norms that "weaken" her position as a woman to backchannel power in equal but different ways. For example, she is likely to set the tone of sexual intimacy, amicability, and overall headship in the relationship as a quid pro quo to the fulfillment of his role as provider and protector. Women therefore hope to strike a balance of what she sees as manhood: 1) a financially adept male that protects her "weaker" state of existence, 2) demonstrates restraint and proper governance over her, and 3) acknowledges her strengths and intellectual capacity.
- Six, a significant portion of her power comes from her ability to evaluate and reward his manhood. She garners power by steering the man's behavior regarding the very

same power of provision and protection he seeks. In her perceived weaker role, she has the power to assess and define his manhood based on the quality of provision and protection he provides. In fact, it is justifiable for her to exit the relationship if he is not providing to her liking, in spite of her ability to be gainfully employed and possibly generate a greater income.

- Seven, her employment does not calculate into the equation of provision and protection. We have often heard the colloquial statement: "What's his is hers and what's hers is hers." Overall, the power of the woman in the Provision-to-Power Theory sediments in her ability to define and shape the identity of his manhood based on her standards of what provision and protection ought to be while 1) maintaining an existential role of the same requirements, 2) upholding her social norm of domestic duties, procreation, and sexual exchange as the pseudo-weaker mate, 3) while maintaining the full capacity to garner economical capital through gainful employment, innovation, and leadership. In practice, this category of women does not actually "submit" to men as the head of the house. Rather, they vie for a space to be heard, acknowledged, and play a significant role in the decision-making process, in other words lead (although they do not refer to these behaviors as leadership).

In essence, the Provision-to-Power Theory reveals a paradox. What is intended as the man's claim to headship over the woman and family also provides women the context by which she helps to define and shape the identity of manhood and masculinity. When weaponized, she is able to undermine and emasculate his headship for failure to "provide" as stated within this social construct of romantic relationships. The paradox further contains a two-way swinging door of potential conflict and violence that exist on both the female and male ends.

- On his side of the door, provision creates a pathway to domination, hyper-masculinity, and control over the woman. I believe many men grow to resent their position as provider because they have found it does not necessarily garner them a satisfying feeling of headship, authority, and autonomy. Men often find themselves struggling with their wife over headship or leadership as he discovers that the verbal recognition of headship does not necessarily translate into practice for many women. These women have dominating personalities and wrestle to see who "wears the pants" in the relationship. Such resentment from a loss or lack of power may lead to dominating and hyper-masculine responses from men.
- On the other side of the paradox, women have a social green light to hold men's feet to the role of provision. As his identity is tied to provision, woe is he who does not follow through. His shortcomings as provider, on her side of the door, creates a pathway for her to demonize, emasculate, and ostracize him. In effect, he is only declared a man if she deems him so. In other words, her ability to evaluate your manhood is more powerful than your ability to meet "her" standards of provision. Your ability to provide must contend with her expectations of provision. Severe emotional violence hangs in the balance with this power for the men who dominate women and the women who emasculate men.

Power, the ability to control and influence an outcome, does not necessarily come with the title of husband (headship or leadership), albeit there is a lingering notion that under the guise of submission, as the man, he should be the more influential entity. That is a smoke screen. A man does not have more power than the woman in the relationship. However, much of the social normative practices places only a greater level of accountability onto him. Headship reflects accountability. This too is another part of the paradox wherein the man looks to have control and influence, yet finds himself less influential and with only more accountability than her. In effect, the man has less power, but more accountability.

This occurs because her ability to provide is not evaluative. Traditional social norms maintain that her financial contribution is additional income, not the main income. This creates another gridlock that narrows the bell curve and widens the conflict zones on male and female ends. In the 21ST century, many women want access to means of provision (education, equal pay, fair opportunity to upward mobility), but sidestep the accountability within relationships. In short, they want the access but not the responsibility. Tradition then becomes the problem as many women practice a-la-carte feminism, picking and choosing what is to their convenience from practices that are no longer sustained by our economic, political, and social climate. Women such as these enforce the role of provision as male because it leaves them in a seat of power (as the enforcer and dictionary of the man's identity), leaving her more affluent and less accountable.

BEING A PURPOSE-DRIVEN MAN

CHAPTER 7

My childhood was relatively normal with the exception of one catastrophic act. I was molested at the age of nine by an older boy in my church over a fateful summer in 1990 for nearly three months. It was a quiet, deep hurt that loomed in my psyche for most of my childhood. I rarely felt comfortable in my own skin while growing up. I often overcompensated amongst my peers in middle school and high school for an emotional injury I did not know how to quite deal with. Undergraduate college, on the other hand, was my refuge. I flourished academically and socially. It was a period of enlightenment and newly found validation that helped me develop a strong sense of self. I had found numerous successes in and out of the classroom as an active student on campus in intramurals, student government, and other student organizations.

After a few years of working in my profession and completing my master's degree, I got married and unfortunately, quickly felt like my nine-year-old self again: lost, unvalidated, confused, and inadequate. Why did I get married? But long before a wife came into the picture, I should have been able to answer some prerequisite questions: "Who am I?" "What is the meaning of my life?" "Why am I here?" And, ultimately, "What is my purpose?" I am now asking you. What do you answer when asked these questions? These are questions you should seek answers to for yourself before seeking a spouse.

Purpose is found in the pool of self-discovery, but you have to be willing to get wet and learn how to swim. This clarity lends itself to a sense of self that brings a peace of mind and emotional balance. But how do you find the answers to these questions? There is no one answer to how you find the answers, but there are things to consider that will help you narrow the scope of your purpose. In order to find your purpose, you have to pull away from the social norms that have already compartmentalized your life, specifically the way in which you define your masculinity, sense of power, and identity. You have to break routine and identify a time and space for reflection, introspection, and listening to your inner voice.

What is purpose? It is important to understand that purpose is not necessarily what you dream of becoming or the dream job you have in mind. On numerous occasions I have heard professional athletes say they found their purpose after retirement from their athletic career. The job you work may finance your purpose, but your purpose is usually not the job you work until it becomes the *job you work*. Purpose is your divine station in life that reflects your greatest sense of self, proving to be your greatest contribution to society. Identifying your purpose should be promoted above simply being a provider. Better yet, we steward best through our purpose. Purpose is an intrinsic compass, which when followed leads you to a promised land of impact, influence, and productivity. Be a purpose-driven man, nothing more and nothing less.

Your purpose may or may not amass financial wealth, but it will leave you so fulfilled, enriched, and empowered that you will leave a deeply profound impression on the lives around you. Purpose walkers lead sustainable works in their families and communities. Purpose walkers amass social wealth for the betterment of themselves, their family, and their community. Purpose walkers understand who they are, embrace the process of growth, and feel uneasy about life until they walk into that silver lining of purpose. Purpose walkers maximize their impact to the most deserving populations. Purpose walkers align their role in the storybook of life to the purpose of others at a specific place and time.

The nucleus of your purpose is often a singular, laser-focused assignment. This does not mean you will not have other roles, such as father, husband, entrepreneur, singer and writer. More importantly, the nucleus of your purpose will serve as a conduit for other roles in your life. How you demonstrate, activate, and participate in that purpose may also be seasonal. For example, I am a conflict resolution practitioner and leadership development trainer. My identity is wrapped in my ability to be a conduit to conflict resolution, specifically in the covert ways in which they present themselves in society. I understand that I must first BE this person for myself before I can be this for others. Next, as my identity is tied to my purpose, the nucleus of my purpose is expressed through being an author, consultant, and educator/trainer. I also coordinate events that are tied to my purpose, such as the EmpowerMEN

Conference, focused on transforming the identity of men in the 21ST century through leadership development and conflict resolution skill building. The combination of your central purpose serves justice for the other areas of your life. In my purpose, I model being a character driven, accountable individual to my children, staff, employers, family and friends. Like anything else worth being, it comes with mistakes, opportunities for growth, and a sense of accomplishment.

DOMESTICATION OF MEN

The term *domestication* in marriage is usually associated with the duties of the household, usually reserved for a woman. Amongst a laundry list of things (pun intended), duties include cooking, cleaning, ironing, and mothering young children. Domestication for men is usually described as the act of getting married. No longer a bachelor, he is now relegated to the responsibilities of married life. On the other hand, gender roles for men in a marriage are not typically discussed as domestication. But I beg to differ. Men experience domestication as do women. While the domestic role of a woman predominates the household, the domestic role of a man is working. Men are taught a lot of things, but the resounding message is that a *real* man is a working man. Some would even capitulate a real man works *by any means necessary*. This often leads to the quiet, unstated pressure and feeling that the sum total of a man is to get a paycheck and provide financially for his family. The truth is men are not simply paychecks. To consider yourself as a financier oversimplifies and masks the true purpose of who you are. Greatness has never had a salary.

DREAMS VS. PURPOSE

We are often encouraged to dream big and go for it. But dreams are often settled in the comfort of society's luxury, such as homes, cars, and riches or maybe even a dream job. There is nothing wrong with dreaming. However, I draw a distinction between purpose and dreams to ensure the person's desire is not skewed. Purpose is who you are. Dreams tend to be who you want to be—unless you are dreaming to be who you are. Nonetheless, do not dream of stardom; dream of finding your purpose in life.

HOW DO YOU FIND YOUR PURPOSE?

Trying to find your purpose may feel like you are chasing a shifty little critter that runs you through the woods bent forward, arms outstretched, always appearing really close to your fingertips. And although you stumble over twigs and lose your footing in the muddy terrain, you keep chasing that little critter until you finally get your hands around its squiggly little body and cage it.

Finding your purpose is a quiet but active process. It requires asking a lot of questions about life and listening for those answers in silence and observation. Purpose is sometimes stumbled upon. Purpose is often the gift that comes naturally to you that just needs to be pointed in the right direction, cultivated, and given the proper amount of motivation, and off you go. Purpose is not singular in design. Purpose is multi-dimensional and creates synergy across relationships.

SPOUSE FOR YOUR PURPOSE

It is a question that pops up quite often at relationship forums: "When do you know you're ready for marriage?" The answer to this question contains a lot of dynamics. Some people may view readiness as being emotionally prepared, financially prepared, career and educationally prepared, or spiritually prepared. Some believe that a man is ready after his wild oats have been sown (as if the woman does not have wild oats that are also sown). I believe a combination of these things must be in play before marriage seems appropriate. More important than those things, knowing and understanding your purpose provides clarity in the selection of a spouse. It also helps you place more emphasis on her character to assess how she fits into or supports your purpose. Could any other woman have supported Martin Luther King Jr.'s purpose better than Coretta Scott King? I do not know MLK Jr.'s process for selecting a spouse, nor do I know the inner workings of their marriage, but the national and global platform triumphed by MLK Jr. could not have occurred without an understanding wife who added to his purpose. Purpose is gender neutral and a requirement of both parties. Both men and women must identify their purpose before marriage.

What happens when purposes between husbands and wives seem to clash? If God is not the author of confusion, then the culture of effective communication must come into play with thorough discussions on developing a plan of support.

SOLUTION BRIDGE

WHY ARE YOU EVEN GETTING MARRIED?

CHAPTER 8

Marriage is a social norm and a rite of passage common to most cultures. Almost every group of people exist under some kind of mutual contract between man and woman that acknowledges them as a formal or legal couple within their society. For many, marriage is an intrinsic part of their life process. At one point, growing up in the church, the immense preaching and construct of God and the church, man and woman, and the bridegroom and the bride left me with a clear understanding that marriage was an inevitable goal. To not aim for marriage would almost seem blasphemous.

Men and women are motivated by many reasons to get married. Some people often tie their social identity to the title of husband or wife as a feeling of accomplishment. For some women, the tradition of their culture expects them to remain at home under the care of their father until marriage, making marriage a strong motivation for the sake of leaving their father's home. For some women, there is a sense of pride in telling others they are married. In many cultures, marriage establishes womanhood. Men have similar points of pride as well. Some men marry to reflect a social status and corporate image. Some cultures believe manhood is ascertained through marriage. Some men and women marry because they want to avoid having children out of wedlock. However, many people marry simply for the sake of marriage as a next natural step in adulthood. The socializing process to marry makes the desire to do so as easy as breathing (until you discover you are emotionally asthmatic).

Marriage on the basis of love is actually a more recent phenomenon over the past 200 years. For centuries prior, people married for upward mobility, survival, and alliance of families for business or political gain. Nowadays, we more frequently cite "love" as a strong component to why people marry. Note, many cultures still practice arranged marriages that have a specific business or political intention.

I believe *love plus purpose* is a good starting ground for marriage. The challenge lies in how we define love and, in many instances, knowing what unconditional love looks like. Love is often a process that may require parts of you to develop and grow for the benefit of your marriage. Additionally, most human development theorists can properly deduce that we all need to feel a sense of belonging and love, and marriage is a great opportunity for us to satisfy those spiritual, emotional, and physical needs. But the question is: why do you want to get married (and stay married)? Note the distinction. What is your motivation?

- Have you been dating a woman for a length of time and marriage seems like a natural next step?
- Have you always looked forward to being a husband?
- Have you been pulled to the side by a church member or church leader and advised to marry because you are sexually involved with her?
- Do you enjoy the sex you are having with her and on your own decided you want to make this permanent?
- Has she asked where this relationship is going, making you feel obligated to marry?
- Have you been with her for over three, five, or seven years and you want to make an "honest woman" out of her?
- Has she given you an ultimatum by requesting you get married soon or end the relationship altogether?
- Do your parents have an expectation for grandchildren and believe marriage should come first, then babies?
- Have you impregnated a woman and decided to not have a child out of wedlock?
- Have you found the woman of your dreams and you are wildly in love with her?
- Did the love of your life slip away before and you are now determined to never let that happen again?
- Have you decided to "man up" and fully commit to her?
- Do you enjoy companionship and the idea of being alone is not a fulfilling idea?
- Do you enjoy the quality of woman she is and see her adding value to your life?
- Have you decided you want a family and she is an ideal person with whom to build a future?
- Do you have business plans and are looking for a partner

that you can trust and see marriage as a conduit to growing your enterprise?

- While you ponder those questions, also consider: Do you know why she wants to marry you?

LEGACY

I believe our most compelling reason for marriage is to build legacy. Legacy instills the fortitude of longevity across generations. Legacy is neutral; it reflects only the qualitative and quantitative output of those who have established it. The legacy of terrorists leaves a long tale of destruction, while the legacy of Civil Rights leaders leaves a long tale of triumph for human rights. Even in the space of not identifying your purpose, you leave a lackluster legacy. We all leave a legacy of one kind or the other.

Legacy starts with first being a purpose-driven man. Legacy is linked to our spaces, environments and the quality of relationships we have built within our sphere of influence, which is best demonstrated through alignment with our purpose. It is not one act, but the sum total of your character and deeds. Legacy is the imprint we leave on the world. In the process of operating within our purpose, we are able to cultivate and build a personal and professional legacy. For those of us fortunate enough to have a biological legacy through our offspring, we are able to pass our legacy on to them.

In building your legacy, know that your livelihood is YOUR responsibility. Your academic and professional pursuits are not for your family, they are for you. Your family will benefit from your success, but your pursuits are part of your individual legacy. You have to identify and walk in your purpose and do the necessary self-development to maintain a sustainable lifetime—this is yours and nobody else's. However, your inner circle of confidants, including your spouse, must add to or complement your purpose and your inevitable legacy. With this said, how do you select your spouse?

HOW TO SELECT A SPOUSE

While in undergrad, my college mentor told me the most important decision I will make in life is selecting a wife. I underestimated his words, but have circled back to understanding the gravity, caution, prayer, and introspection required in this process. The selection of your wife is a very careful matter because your spouse reflects who you are. How then do you choose? Even in religious circles you may hear different feedback on how to approach selecting a wife. I grew up in a church that advocated God reveals to you through prayer exactly who your spouse is. On the other hand, I have heard other pastors adamantly preach that God does not select your spouse, you do. One preacher contended that if God selected your spouse then you would blame God for the things that went wrong in the marriage because, after all, God gave you this person.

I married my wife at the time under a strong conviction that God had given her to me as my wife. My process had included speaking to my pastors for clarity and agreement. Additionally, I wanted a family and someone who shared those family expectations and values, which she did. I was certain she was the one to marry after two of my church leaders had returned to me saying their prayer and visions had confirmed her as my wife-to-be. With that expressed agreement, I ignored the signs, which hindsight shows ever so clearly, that might have prevented me from such a blind-sighted marriage.

While going through my divorce, I would often question if it was truly the perfect will of God for us to marry. Now facing an impending divorce, a third pastor shared his spiritual insight with me. He said that my wife at the time was of my choosing and it was never God's will for me to marry her. The implication was that I had endured a tumultuous marriage because I had married outside the will of God. The contrasting feedback from what the other pastors shared prior to marriage versus what I was hearing left me confused. I spewed great accusations to God for being so cruel to me. Already experiencing the pain of separation and impending divorce, my spiritual world was further shaken with more uncertainty about what and who to believe.

With spirituality as such a major component of many of our lives, the feedback from spiritual leaders can have a tremendous effect on us. And with diverging points in the religious community on how to select a spouse, how then do you choose? Choosing a wife is like trying to find a specific needle in a haystack of needles. From my experience, I have derived that alignment of the following three things are necessary in selecting your spouse: 1) awareness of maturity, 2) preparing behaviors, and 3) spiritual aptitude.

AWARENESS OF MATURITY

A mature person can recognize the immaturity in another person. Maturity is gained over time and through experiences. You have to be able to adequately assess yourself and your potential wife's level of maturity. Her maturity level (and yours) will greatly affect how the two of you communicate to each other and manage the needs of the relationship. My wife at the time was 22 years of age, had never lived on her own, had never managed more bills than her cell phone payment, and was at the very beginning of her professional career. She was extremely inexperienced and unexposed to a lot of real-world experiences. Her maturity level was very low. And I failed to recognize and acknowledge it accordingly.

You have to gauge the maturity level of your potential wife and determine where she is transparent in her need to grow in certain areas and then gauge her willingness to learn. The same goes for you. Do you have the prerequisite training and experience that helps you understand the nuances of sharing and managing the life of another human being? And if you do not, how do you gain those experiences? Are you willing to learn, and is she willing to work with you through the learning process and vice-versa? The larger impact of maturity is assessed through your willingness to be patient with the learning and growing process as your wife-to-be or current wife may not be maturing as fast as you desire. Maturity is also a process of self-discovery that leads to understanding one's purpose. Select a spouse according to the purpose of your life. And as much as you can, do not choose one until your purpose is discovered.

Preparing Behaviors

When having the conversation with her parents about my desire to marry their daughter, her mother stated, "She's not ready for marriage." My commitment to the desire to marry undermined her mother's words. Nonetheless, after getting married, I recommended to my wife at the time that we should spend the next year getting to know each other as a married couple. I specifically shared that I desired for the two of us to educate ourselves on how marriages succeed and fail so we could buffer ourselves against the pitfalls ahead. While this may have been better served prior to marriage,

I thought it was not too late to start this process. Unfortunately, she adamantly declined and expressed greater interest in her education and career. How we are least educated and prepared for one of the most important decisions we make, getting married, has always baffled me.

Preparedness for marriage is a culmination of spiritual, emotional, physical, financial, and educational preparedness. How a person gets married and remains married has to go beyond the direct and indirect social cues we have experienced. Real signs of preparedness include marriage counseling and studying the art of marriage through books, seminars, and conferences, not just prayer and desire alone. Preparedness also includes the emotional maturity necessary to allow another person into your life. How well are you able to identify preparing behaviors in your potential wife? What are your preparing behaviors as you move toward becoming a husband? The process of preparing reflects maturity and helps to emotionally and spiritually equip you for marriage.

SPIRITUAL APTITUDE & AGREEMENT

The spiritual aptitude is the culmination of the maturity level, preparedness, attitude toward learning and sharing, and cues that confirm or negate the decision to marry expressed by you and your significant other. It is a reliance on your internal sensibilities that informs you whether something is right or wrong about the road toward marriage. Your spiritual aptitude is your personal undertaking to ensure your decision in spite of agreement from your church leaders or the consensus from family and friends. Your spiritual aptitude is your Spidey senses that tingle as it observes new behaviors or occurrences that would otherwise go unnoticed or unchecked by you or her. While seeking spiritual counsel is productive, your spiritual aptitude places the decision-making power back in your hands.

As my marriage at the time came to an end, I came to the grueling realization that the most perfect design can change because we are dealing with imperfect people. After much back and forth and prayer, I am at peace in believing that my wife and I at the time were perfectly joined together. The problem is that I may have been the only one who believed it. During the divorce process, my wife at the time admitted two crucial things that placed the nine years of marriage into perspective. First, she acknowledged that she'd checked out of the marriage after the first five months. Second, she told me she married me because I was a handsome, professional, Christian, Black man. Knowing this explained a lot, if not everything, including the way she talked and treated me from very early in the marriage. However, the signs of her no longer being in agreement to marry were there prior to marriage. Instead of understanding the significance of the signs, I assumed she would change or that God would work it out. I remained married to someone who had divorced me in their heart after five months. To remain married to her after her expressed disagreement with the divine word may be the space where I chose to marry outside the will of God, because the lack of agreement changed the agreement.

It is true that you and this woman, spoken from the Heavens by God himself, are perfect for each other. But are the two of you willing to walk in agreement in the perfection and purpose of your union? Two cannot walk together unless they agree. And you cannot have two masters as you will love one and hate the other. Do you and your potential wife agree with the spoken word of your union? Do you and your potential wife serve one master of selflessness toward each other? Your spiritual aptitude should recognize these shifts in the relationship. The next steps would involve wisely responding to what your spiritual observations are signaling.

CONFLICTS, COMMUNICATION, AND CONDEMNATION IN MARRIAGES

CHAPTER 9

I quickly discovered a serious pet peeve when I first got married to my wife at the time: high-heeled shoes left lying around the house with the shoe facing down and the heel sticking up. I would always ask her to pick her shoes up and put them away. One evening while walking with a plate of food to the couch, I nearly stepped on the heel with my bare foot. I felt the heel begin to penetrate the bottom of my left foot. I quickly made an extra hop on my other foot to keep my balance and not step down on the heel any further. I was livid. I wanted to break every heel off every shoe she had. I snapped at her because now I had almost hurt myself. I was in my feelings, mostly because I felt as if she paid little regard to my efforts to keep our home clean and just left her shoes anywhere. Over the years of marriage, I ranted about her not being a tidy person. Conflicts tend to carry conversations that condemn as we play judge and jury over our spouse. Wrong or right for leaving the shoes out, the important part of the conflict was how it was resolved. It would have profited me more to simply pick up her shoes. And even on occasions when I did pick them up and organize her closet (at least twice), my attitude of contempt trumped my actions of good will. Marriages are frequently challenged with conflict, communication breakdowns, and condemnation that stem from the least of things to the gravest of issues.

CONFLICTS

Marriage merges the physical, emotional, and spiritual lives of two people, who bring with them tons of known and hidden motives and values. Oftentimes, people do not know how they will react in a situation until they are confronted with it. On any given Sunday, something can hit the fan: a co-worker has some jarring words, in-laws unexpectedly come into town, a car with mechanical problems, emotional flares from a past abusive encounter, feelings of insecurities or inadequacies, personal weight loss goals that can never seem to start, and pressure from multiple sources at once including work and home. As a husman (husband + man), you also have your own personal battles in addition to the potential of any of the above mentioned springing up as an issue.

Conflict also occurs when goals, perceptions, and meta-values are different. This can show up in childrearing decisions, views on domestic duties, communication style, and conflict resolution styles amongst many other things. Conflict also shows up in the little foxes of the marriage, such as the proverbial toilet seat being left up; eating in the bed and leaving crumbs; sleeping with the television on versus sleeping in complete darkness; where clothes are left after disrobing; where shoes are placed; snoring; hogging the bedsheets; house temperature too hot or cold; too many lights on in unoccupied parts of the home; pornography; showering with the water on while soaping up; using all the hot water in the shower; peeing in the shower; rinsing out the tub after showering or bathing; procrastinating; forgetfulness; getting out of shape; spending most of the time with the children; leaving dirty dishes in the sink after the kitchen has been cleaned; leaving clothes in the dryer; stuffing your drawer with clothes instead of folding them; smacking your gum; making the food too salty or without enough seasoning; leaving the toothpaste cap off; leaving a wet floor after coming out of the shower; tracking mud into the house with a dirty shoe; going to bed without showering; leaving the refrigerator door open for extended periods; farting; burping; late night requests for food; late night requests for sex; and the list goes on. Welcome to the daily routine of marriage. You are now two pieces of iron being forged in the fire.

CONVERSATIONS & CONDEMNATION

"Sticks and stones may break my bones, but words can never hurt me." Not true. This adage is false beyond false. Words hurt. And oftentimes they hurt more than sticks and stones. People frequently hurl words that condescend, discourage and condemn. Our voice is the most important aspect of our existence and people can spend more time sparring with fighting words than physically being combative. Everything we do vocalizes, including our behavior at various levels and in various ways based on their social and cultural norms and personal practices. Quite often the war amongst people is intended to silence another person or group's voice. In politics, groups of people are silenced through lack of representation; in housing, people are silenced through redlining; in economics people are silenced through lack of access to funding; in marriage, spouses are silenced when their feelings, perspectives, and experiences are overlooked or dismissed. In other words, when the leadership capacity of the individual in the relationship is undermined or overlooked, conflict is likely to happen.

If we understand the importance of our voice, how then can words "never hurt"? Words are the epitome of legislation, written and stated. Every human being legislates themselves through their values and beliefs presented through their social, cultural, and personal practices. We also legislate ourselves in marriage beginning with the marital vows and other do's and don'ts. In effect, our voice, and the various ways in which we verbally, non-verbally, socially, and culturally communicate have severe consequences or rewards for marriages.

RESPONSIBLE WORDS

Words have a responsibility to fulfill every time they are spoken. Words are also meant to create understanding and relay emotion. Life and death are therefore in the tongue. Words can be heard, felt, and even seen. In a conversation over the phone, you can hear, feel, and even picture the grimace in the person's voice as they tell you a story of betrayal. On a brighter side, you can hear the joy and hear the smile of a person excited about finishing medical school. Barking the words "I love you" relays an emotion that makes the words not feel believable. Saying, "I love you" calmly and smoothly communicates a sense of truth and sincerity. Words are not *just* words; words carry energy. The chanting of your name from an arena full of fans is electrifying, sending sound waves of energy that feed the energy of your physical, emotional, and spiritual being. Words carry energy. What is given to armies before going into war, before sports teams take the field, before the sales team takes to the phones, and after an achievement has been awarded? A speech. Words to validate the people and affirm the mission and vision.

Audio can be measured as sound waves and the sound barrier indicates the speed of sound. Sound has a speed! Speed has a force! Force has momentum! In other words, words move people, and in that movement, words can be CPR to a failing spirit or the knife into a vulnerable lung. Because words have a responsibility, they in effect have the ability to only do one of two things: give life or kill (Proverbs 18:21).

My pastor often reprimanded me (and rightfully so) for speaking death into my marriage at the time by speaking harshly, begrudgingly, or judgmentally against my wife. Her words of wrath were met with my words of wrath. Arguments, by year three of our marriage and for the remainder of the marriage, were intended to see who could cut the deepest. The marriage had started with immense verbal abuse from her and ended with a toxic cycle of verbal abuse.

It is hard to take words back after they have been said. Trying to take words back is like trying to push a newborn back into the womb. That baby of verbal death is here. You have to deal with it, own it, raise it, and try to correct it. That is why love and forgiveness are so important and are said to be for you and not the person who harmed you, because an apology does not easily undo hurtful words. Healing does occur over time with diligent and faithful actions that demonstrate sincerity and commitment to the marriage. But avoiding the onslaught of deadly verbal communication is the way to initially manage your marriage.

CULTURE OF AFFIRMING COMMUNICATION

It's often said the key to a successful relationship is communication. My father says communication is not the key because people talk too much—I think he's on to something. I have found it to be a combination of two things that make communication a poor key to success in relationships: 1) we tend to be overly communicative, and 2) what we say, when we say it, and how we say it makes all the difference in the effectiveness of our communication. Communication is also hampered by a lack of active listening skills and failure to comprehend the multidimensional conversations all happening at once. These elements make all the difference in being an effective communicator.

TIMING IN COMMUNICATION

When to speak is just as important as what to say. Timing is a matter of wisdom. The interesting thing about marriage is that anytime can be the wrong time to talk about a concern you have. Before work? After work? Before going to bed or while in bed? After the kids are in bed? During dinner? How about right now? What about later? During her lunch break? During your lunch break? Maybe on the drive to church? Two days from now? After she's off her cycle? Maybe this weekend? Or at the very moment you muster up the willingness to have the conversation? When is the best time to have the conversation? However, the issue is not so much a matter of timing but more so a matter of culture. Culture is a way of life. You therefore have to create a culture of affirming communication in the relationship.

If your communication always seeks to encourage, uplift, and affirm, then conversations about a concern you have should follow suit. The culture of affirming communication is built over time and serves as a strategy to combat words of death. The most important part of this process is making sure you're with a woman you truly want to invest your spiritual, emotional, and physical energy into. You get better results when you genuinely desire to love and see your loved one in a space of harmony. But you must first know who you are, be transparent and authentic to yourself, and live a purpose-filled life. When you, man and husband, are operating in that space, your culture of affirming communication is built on the mission and vision of the marriage, requiring you to see your wife as essential to that process. In seeing the importance of her role in your life, you therefore build her as she builds you. You might have moments of being upset, displeased, irritated, or annoyed by your spouse. However, the problem is not the problem; how you manage the problem is always 99 percent of the issue.

TONE OF VOICE

I'm not too concrete on the matter of tone of voice. I often find the choice of tone subjective to how an individual wants to be spoken to. Sometimes a person with a harsh sounding tone is just talking how they talk and don't mean anything else by it. Other people may recoil. Some people may be receptive to this tone of voice. However, our word choice tends to dictate our tone. As I mentioned before, saying "I love you" tends to carry a calmness and smoothness that echoes sincerity. And when engaged in a heated argument, words of anger tend to carry a loud, heavy, sharp tone of voice. Of course, you also have the sweet tone of voice that curses and cuts you sideways without raising a decibel. As such, it's hard to judge tone of voice as a proper barometer of a person's heart. Nonetheless, communication with your wife should not tear her down or destroy her. She reflects who you are, and as my pastor told me countless times, what you say about her are things you're also saying about yourself.

Communication Skills Are Taught

A major reason why we overly and ineffectively communicate is because most people simply haven't been taught how to be skillful communicators. Communication breakdowns happen all the time in the blink of a word. Being well-spoken or college-educated doesn't translate into effective communication that helps you resolve conflict. I've had to learn that my ability to communicate well in a corporate setting did not necessarily translate into the communication required for my spouse. Communication training in school teaches public speaking, how to frame persuasive arguments, and debate techniques. However, in everyday living, those skills are reserved for the classroom, debate club, and politics. While the formal lessons are instructive, they don't necessarily work for marriage, especially when emotions are running high from the personal investments you have made in each other. School doesn't teach you how to speak *Womanese*, and more specifically the dialect of your wife. Speaking the dialect of your wife is just another way of saying building the culture of effective communication between you and her in a way that supports healthy conversations, something that is done over time.

LISTENING TO UNDERSTAND

I did not know how to effectively communicate with my wife at the time. My mathematical-logical brain often stood in front of my sensitivity. She would cautiously introduce conversations with statements like, "This isn't easy for me to talk about," or "I don't like having these conversations," or "Can I talk to you about something and can you just hear me out first?" Even still, her best attempts to have a conversation with me about something that she had a lot of emotions behind were oftentimes met with my overly rational and logical response. Many times, in my mind, I had already resolved the problem and was just waiting for her to finish talking to unveil a solution. I would often cut her off by starting to ask questions with an intention to see if my microwave answer was going to be appropriate. Ultimately, I was not a safe place with whom to communicate, not because I demonized her, but because I did not support her by actively listening and allowing her the opportunity to talk about the process she was going through. That feeling of not feeling safe creates a trickle-down effect of losing trust. After all, no other place should be ideal for her to go than sharing with her husband. It's important to learn that when your wife is speaking her heart you should not be speaking your mind. **It's important to develop active listening skills and a feedback system that works for your marriage.**

Husbands and wives tend to share their deep emotions, concerns, and perspectives with each other. In a very short time you get a good sense of how each other manages life by living and sharing space. You get to see the character, behavior, and human side of your spouse's day-to-day life. Life is a process of continual learning, growing, trial and error, reinvention, and testing of the will. Neither of you will have it all figured out. Conflict is inevitable when the expectation to know, the responsibility to figure it out, and accountability of the outcome rests largely on one person's shoulder.

You have to be prepared for your spouse to tell you anything regarding their deep feelings or emotions, knowing that you are a safe haven for her to share and not be condemned. Furthermore, be prepared for her thoughts and feelings to change as she matures with experience and growth in her spirituality, emotions, and physicality. The following can assist in creating a culture of affirming communication:

1. Ask your wife what is the best way to communicate to her.
2. Ask your wife when is the best time for the both of you to communicate.
3. Be honest and transparent.
4. Make it clear that you want to solve the problem.
5. Give her lots of booty rubs.
6. Ask to try out different strategies to solve a problem.
7. Always speak in complimentary terms.
8. Always affirm your spouse with words of encouragement that remind them of their strength and ability to be successful in any matter.
9. Rub her booty.
10. Celebrate the success of your spouse through gift giving or moments of acknowledgment.

THE NEED TO BE RIGHT

Creating a culture of effective communication requires you to purge and eradicate the *need to be right*. The *need to be right* comes from a disease worse than leprosy, the plague, the AIDS epidemic, and swine flu. It's an ailment that has brought down mankind for as far back as history allows us to go. It's called the ego; some call it pride. The *need to be right* wins the battle but creates distance between you and your wife. Rest assured that nothing is wrong with being right. The downfall comes in the *need* to be right. The *need* can lead to a poor attitude, misbehaviors, and deadly words of communication.

While my wife at the time was finishing graduate school, I had a vision of her being an entrepreneur. I didn't know what type of business, but I could see it as clearly as it was revealed. She and I had recently met a woman who wanted her to get involved in a business. But my wife at the time was not interested. I shared with my wife that I saw entrepreneurialism in her future and encouraged her to meet with the lady and find out more about the opportunity. My wife at the time snapped back with some harsh words about her own intentions for her future. She made it clear to not tell her what to do. I was taken aback by her response because I was trying to be encouraging and empowering. On this rare occasion I actually had no response. It may have been four years later, but one day I received a text message from her saying, "I guess you were right. I am an entrepreneur." By now she had finished graduate school and met her goal of three children before the age of 30. Now she could see herself starting her own business. In fact, she started three. Time proved me right. However, it took a lot for me to receive that text message and not dig up the past about how she'd spoken to me that day in order to highlight how right I was. I learned from that experience that time will prove you right or wrong.

It's okay to be wrong. And it's okay to not be right, right now. Every word we speak out of our mouth has a responsibility to fulfill. The beauty in that is time will prove truths to be truths and lies to be lies. Time will also allow us the space to correct mistakes. As mentioned above, time proved that the God-sent vision I had of her to be true. And as fate would have it, she turned out to be a very creative and intelligent entrepreneur.

SEX IN THE MARRIAGE

CHAPTER 10

At a certain point in my marriage at the time, sex had become complicated and in some instances was being used as a weapon. My request to make love was often denied and met with the usual rhetoric of being tired, preoccupied, or simply not in the mood. My wife at the time once said she felt as if I *only* wanted her for sex. That was a farce. I guess the house, car, management of bills, cleaning, and fathering was for sex only too.

Whether for recreation or procreation, sexual lovemaking is vitally important to a marriage. Like any matter that can become a potential conflict such as finances or childrearing decisions, how we are socialized about sex can easily distort or destroy a healthy relationship with our spouse. Sex is a spiritual, emotional, and physical undertaking that binds two people together in ways that deeply impact the consenting parties. In sexual lovemaking, you share and exchange the essence of who you are to the point that it can produce life—that's powerful.

It's avowed that men are visually, sexually charged creatures who, in many of their endeavors, position themselves to mate with a woman. It has been stated that men's motivation for achieving financial success, driving fancy cars, dressing nicely, and even acting macho are peacocking attempts to prove himself an alpha male with sexual conquest as a winning prize. However, women are just as sexual as men. Unfortunately, our social order has historically suppressed the sexual expression of women, often relegating the woman to a sexually-objectified space, while ignoring her sexual desires. Nonetheless, at the end of the day, in general, men and women enjoy lots of sex. But like most things between men and women, our approach to sex is slightly different. Unfortunately, *slightly* in a marriage can mean miles of differences.

A CONNECTING TOOL

Fortunately, it was not the case that I *only* wanted sex from my wife at the time. What I did not know was how to communicate that I wanted to connect. I wanted to get to know her while getting to know her. In other words, I wanted to simultaneously get to know her spiritually, emotionally, and physically. No part of me desired to just stick it in and pump away. I wanted to create a space of love-making and connection—it was important to me.

Sex for a woman is usually described as an emotional undertaking. On the other hand, for men, sex is often described as simply a physical act—again, putting men into an unemotional box. Men are emotional about sex. As a human, you are an emotional creature who wants to feel desired and loved. Sex in a loving relationship is one of the greatest methods of bi-lateral communication. Sex between lovers transcends the physical and becomes lovemaking. The same way sex for a woman can be tied to her feelings of security and comfort with her husband, men also share the same need of security and comfort. No gender is exempt. Women and men share the same sentiments regarding sex as human beings share in all emotions. The difference is our conditioning and the words men use when communicating about sex. What men are told and not told about sex contributes significantly to the poor communication some men may experience.

Men don't often talk about lovemaking as a connection tool. The vernacular often used by men about sex may seem too direct or appear to lack an emotional appeal to his female counterpart. But are men taught to view and discuss the deeper spiritual and emotional aspects of sex? No different for a woman, lovemaking for a man is a connection tool, a deep engaging experience, a sacred experience, an expression of love and desire, and a vulnerable moment.

I was also never taught that the physical make-up of an erect penis is a symbol of power between genders. The operative word is erect. Men erect. Erect means to construct, build, establish, and set upright. The posture of an erect man is a symbol of power. A woman submits to this power during sex by allowing him to enter her. No matter how involved a woman is during sex, her vagina is always a receiver of the penis. Sex, therefore, is an act of power, domination, and submission—an exchange between man and woman as they both seek to empower each other through the sexual lovemaking process. Her decision to provide access to her maintains the balance of power.

However, like in any matter, abuse of power is where the problem lies. On one extreme, notwithstanding role-playing for the kinky couples, forcibly having sex with your wife against her will is rape. Albeit your wife, she has a right to say no and so do you. On the other extreme, a wife's repeated decline to her sexual access is a form of sexual abuse. Meanwhile, using the social standard of monogamy to prevent him from stepping outside of the relationship while denying him sexual access within the relationship. Clearly, at this point, the sexual temperature of the marriage is indicative of larger issues plaguing the couple. Note, however, that a woman's truer space of power is her womb, not her vagina. Her womb carries and nurtures life, while her vagina is just the doorway to her sacred womb.

How should sex in marriage be? I Corinthians 7:3-5 says, "Let the husband render unto the wife due benevolence: and likewise, also the wife unto the husband. The wife hath not power of her own body, but the husband: and likewise, also the husband hath not power of his own body, but the wife. Defraud ye not one the other, except it be with consent for a time, that ye may give yourselves to fasting and prayer; and come together again, that Satan tempt you not for your incontinency."

THE POWER DYNAMICS OF SEXUAL CONQUEST

How often are men taught to be sexually modest? On the contrary, men are taught their manhood is defined by their sexual conquests while women are taught their womanhood is defined by their sexual conservativeness. Society simultaneously praises men for their sexual conquests and labels promiscuous women as whores, and then, after years of such indoctrination, demand that men be monogamous creatures with "good girls" who are less experienced in the bedroom.

#failed #thatdoesntmakesense #toomuchcontradiction

We find many points of conflict in the male-female relationship dynamics because women are taught differently from men. The competing curriculum is counterintuitive to holistic living as a married couple. And again, power dynamics become front and center in the sexual space between husband and wife. #teachdifferent #ifwewantdifferent. Men and women should share in the same knowledge base in the effort of raising informed, respectful children into adulthood, both girl and boy, who understand the power of sex and lovemaking. Similar to girls, boys should be taught:

- A mature man practices sexual conservativeness
- The penis is an instrument of power that should be cherished and not easily accessible
- Manhood is not defined by your number of sexual conquests
- A man's body ought to be kept
- Sex is not the end game
- Sex is a responsibility for someone's spiritual, emotional, and physical well-being
- Women can also use men for sex

THE PEN IS

a poem

There's an overwhelming misconception that's been going around
Deep in the soul a couple centuries old that a man only wants to get down
To a large extent it seems to be the case, they say men love to chase
Get home from work, catch a nap, shower, get fresh, and be up in the place
Tongue hanging like the dogs they're said to be, trying to get a taste
Telling the truth divided by two, hoping to impress chicks, wet their sticks, gloss their face
While trying to determine if it's worth their time to continue spending time
Forging opportunities to make the booty wine
After all, she's a dime and some men feel incline, especially when their fine
To spend them pennies to keep as many as they can on the line

How was this notion established?
Did it start in Africa or was it on the ship?
Were Black men told "Negro, I don't need you loving no black trick;
Your job is to breed, pick cotton, and bleed, and give me your off-spring to do as I need"
But it's not just men in America –
Men in Taiwan want the same damn thing
English men use the accent to get some action
French men speak that language of love for the same reaction
And men down under love going down under

But I propose a different take, if you believe in Adam and Eve
Puts it in perspective that it's all about the vitamin D
Fellas don't been tricked, bamboozled for your gift
Deceived into thinking that the Gina is the it
Don't let the lust flip the script
Take our God given authority to rule by the fortitude and power of the stiff
And instead fall prey to deception that they, purport
To let Gina steer the ship
A man's natural resource is worth more than oil pumping –
But some men are quick to cheapen themselves for some booty they see crumping –
Or some female with a tale who can fry a good dumpling

Men, your pen is worth something
A lot more than scribbling; let me give you an inkling
Inside of you is a universe of planets,
Millions of specimen of futures in your container
An erection that erects "in the beginning"
For in the beginning, God created the heavens and the earth
And in you is the same power to create – if you only knew your worth
Gina isn't it – call it a shaft, a pen, a member, a stick
Whatever your metaphor, stop choosing to be a whore
And renew your mind for the reason you met-her-for

I've never met a woman who needed a man for sex
Every sister I've ever met
Needed to be emotionally and spiritually reset
But men are sometimes more interested in giving her the business

Repent – it's hard living a life of sin
Fellas be reserved in how you use your pen –
It's a gift for which she should be honored to get
Women no disrespect,
Your role is important; you're the other half of the piece
But my men need to be reached
So in turn they can return to their women's sheet
And write a story of love and how best friends meet.

LOVEMAKING VERSUS SEX

Lovemaking is the interaction you share in an environment of love on an ongoing, 24-hour basis. When love is the center of your act of service towards your wife, you are making love to her. Washing the dishes, making her laugh, picking up groceries, taking her out, washing her back, putting the kids to bed, catering to your in-laws, and everything else you do throughout the marriage will always be an act of lovemaking. Intercourse is just one facet of lovemaking. You might discover that your wife's deepest orgasm is from something you do that has nothing to do with intercourse.

MANIPULATION, CONTROL, POWER & THE IMPRISONMENT OF SEX

As awesome as the lovemaking process can be, a serious injury to any marriage is when the man or woman uses sex as a means to manipulate, control, or exert power in the relationship. Withholding sex from your wife is a catastrophic move unreflective of love—you cannot be in love and not make love. This has physical and emotional consequences that seep into other aspects of the relationship. And vice versa, other challenges in the marriage may affect the sexual desire for each other.

It is more popularly said that wives withhold sex from their husbands. We refer to it as the switch and bait; plenty of sex prior to marriage followed by a serious drop in libido after the nuptials are consecrated. To forward the belief that the wife usually withholds from her husband further supports the idea that men are the more sexually invested creatures. That is not true, especially in a marriage. Quite often, a woman waits until marriage to be what she considers sexually open. Nonetheless, in or out of marriage, women are equally interested in sex. A divorcing woman expressed to me her frustration with the sexual practices in her marriage saying, "I wish he would have just woken me up with sex. Do that first, and then say good morning. I'll be ready to go make breakfast after that. But he refused to touch me." There are many husbands withholding sex from their wives. Withholding sex by either husband or wife is a demonstration of power and control, thereby making sex in the marriage an opportunity for manipulation and emotional imprisonment. Withholding sex is usually a control tactic requiring a change in behavior before granting access back to lovemaking. Attempting to control a person's behavior by holding hostage their rightful sexual desire toward their spouse is not a loving practice. The only way to make love is to make it.

Furthermore, withholding sex from your spouse is a form of rejection—and no one likes rejection, especially if you view sex as a connecting form of expression. To deny your spouse sex may be seen as a denying of your spouse's self-worth. Sex, a transparent act of submission, places both parties in a very vulnerable space that is easily disrupted by the very thought of no longer feeling desirable. Outside stressors such as work, extended family, or personal insecurities among others factors in the marriage can detract from the sexual lovemaking flame in a marriage. It is understandable that one party may decide against intercourse for that moment. The issue I'm discussing here is not a specific time of isolation, rather, the systematic approach of withholding sex from a spouse, an act of emotional imprisonment.

Imagine if your basic need for water was socially, biblically, religiously, and legally relegated to only one well. To go to another well would be considered in breach of your contract that says you can only dip your bucket into this well. What if your recourse for a well contractually obligated to provide you water has run dry?

Withholding sex from your spouse presents a serious layer of challenge, specifically the challenge of sexual faithfulness to the marriage. Infidelity, a devastating blow to any marriage, occurs for many different reasons under many different circumstances. Infidelity is not always tied to the issue of sexual access to their spouse. Many spouses step outside of the marriage in spite of a very sexually active marriage. However, my specific focus deals with infidelity as a result of a spouse systematically withholding sex. Sex isn't everything, but not having it is. I have always wondered: *If sex was important enough to upend the marriage, why wasn't it important enough to have during the marriage?*

Withholding sex is wrong; infidelity is wrong. Two wrongs do not make a right. However, I contend that the spouse who withholds has committed the greater offense against their husband or wife because of the power, attempt to control, potential to manipulate, and emotional imprisonment that occurs. The withholding party has morally and religiously imprisoned their spouse's appropriate and rightful sexual desire. The rejected spouse is forced to suppress their appropriate sexual desire at the whim of the withholding spouse. Unlike food, if the wife doesn't cook, there is no religious or ethical clause preventing the husband from eating at his neighbors', a local restaurant, or even making his own food. On the other hand, dropping your bucket in another well for water is infidelity and frowned upon to say the least.

HOW CHEATING *REALLY* WORKS

The Cheating Scheme

Infidelity is not a fair demarcation of what is really going on between married couples, but it's a social standard that nearly all religious, political, and social entities agree is unacceptable behavior. However, I do not advocate to not cheat because of its ethical reasons, albeit that is important. I advocate to not cheat because it empowers your significant other to hold a higher moral ground than you in spite of their trespasses in the relationship. In effect, it is a power move used to undermine your credibility as a husband and as a man while she imagines herself as the victim. At the moment you step outside of your relationship, her wrongdoing immediately falls to a distant second place.

Relationships have private hurts and public hurts. Private hurts are the emotional, psychological and physical abuse that occurs behind closed doors. They range from mild to severe. When infidelity comes to light (and it will), it is now a public hurt. Knowledge of your behavior eventually seeps out and other people, including the mistress, friends, family members and trusted confidants, in other words, the public, are now in the know. Women find this shameful. It's a blight on their womanhood that now provides her a social moral high ground that overshadows her wrongdoing.

The public perception of infidelity can be greater than the act itself. My statement here does not promote being more covert in the practice of infidelity. Remember, it eventually comes to light. My rationale here is intended to help you keep the playing field leveled when conflict arises in the relationship. Once infidelity is introduced to the marriage, you lose power. No matter how you justify stepping outside of the relationship, she will most likely lean on the strength of public perception to downplay her emotional, psychological, and physical abuses toward you. What then do you do?

The spouse who has stepped out of the marriage is met with a stigma and labeled as cheater, adulterer, and unfaithful. But what do you label the spouse who withholds sex? Well, that is never really the conversation, is it? Yet it may possibly be the more detrimental act. The social conversation dutifully condemns the adulterer while undermining the impact of the withholder. However, no issue is an island unto itself. Challenges within the marriage easily and quickly feed into other parts of the relationship. When termites eat away at the roofing structure, they impact the structural integrity of the house, which results in a collapsed roof during the rainy season. Nonetheless, don't cheat.

Do not let sex control you. You will discover that when your relationship is on a pathway of "let's get married and do everything except make it last," the smallest of insecurities and distrust can topple the marriage without the added stress of infidelity added to the mix. A casual hello to someone, spending money on a small item, or burping without saying excuse me could be enough to set off an emotionally charged person who already finds you unsatisfactory as a mate. And you might just be an unqualified husband; however, infidelity is just more proof of how unqualified you are. Don't cheat.

Women Cheat Too

Women cheat. And are said to be better at it because they are better at hiding it. This is similar to how white upper-class people are more likely to use and sell drugs, yet, Black male are more likely to be suspected of being drug dealers, which leads to a disproportionate level of police attention on black communities. Women use the social narrative as part to hide their behavior because they are less likely to be suspected of infidelity, allowing them to get away with it more. According to my parenting class trainer, infidelity amongst married couples happens at a 50/50 rate because married men and women tend to cheat with other married men and women.

There is also a tendency for greater empathy toward a wife's infidelity as opposed to men. Another great misnomer is that women (and only women) are likely to cheat because their husband is not emotionally satisfying or connecting with them. And because women, by default (sarcasm), are faithful to their husbands, if a woman cheats, it's most likely because of the emotional neglect she was enduring. This is another example of how our society in many ways has socially compartmentalized women as victims and men as victimizers, making it more easily acceptable to "understand" a woman's infidelity because women are viewed as emotional. Meanwhile, a man's infidelity is deemed as "normal" male behavior because our social conversation reinforces the stigma that men cheat, men get in where they fit in, men think with their head below, and overall, men are sexually motivated with high doses of gullibility. Further cementing the narrative is the caution to women regarding sexually pleasing their husbands: "What she won't do, another woman will." It's also widely stated that men can't handle their woman cheating on them; meanwhile, women are more often forced to have to deal with a cheating husband as she is looked on as a scorned wife. Do you see the tangled web and cycles of conflict our behavior and social conversation creates? It is another conundrum for both men and women.

Another component of this matter is the thinking that the woman is the "good" of the relationship. Scripturally based, it states that when a man finds a wife he finds a good thing. Short-sided hermeneutics draws an oversimplified conclusion, that only the woman is the good thing. Therefore, women are good and men are bad (unfaithful, misogynists, sexually weak). This thinking provides subtle support and subconsciously props up the notion that women are victims and men victimize that "good thing." And with latency further supports the emotional difference in men and women that leads to empathizing a woman's infidelity: the "good thing" would not do something as bad as cheat unless she was severely neglected or emotionally abused.

Also, on the other extreme, where men perpetrate violence against women who have cheated, the same logic applies. The "good thing" is not supposed to act wayward (only the man), therefore, her infidelity is worse and deserves a harsher response. Some cultures support deadly violence against women who have cheated on their spouse. These men make excuses for their waywardness as a predisposition to being a man, while reserving higher standards for the woman as the "good thing." The logic on either side of the discussion is flawed, unfair, and counterproductive to the practice of a healthy union.

Add all of this to the Scripture that describes women as the weaker vessel and you have the perfect playground for patriarchal domination and psychological warfare in defining the identity of women and controlling their behavior. It becomes an atrocity on both sides as men are belabored by the burden to uphold these systems of emotional, psychological, and physical violence toward women and women are forced to live under such duress in which they retaliate with the same violence back on to men.

Emotional infidelity is also a major issue. Emotional infidelity occurs when you befriend, confide, and develop a deepened trust and bond with another woman. The fact is, wrong is wrong. Lack of knowledge or ego may seriously prevent you from seeking help in creating an effective culture of communication, which includes the sexual space you share. Lack of knowledge might make you feel un-empowered. A lot of times, ego digs in its heels and refuses to see how each party is contributing to the other party and refuses to find help.

I understand first-hand the amount of mental and emotional energy required to address an issue that is supposed to be so primal to our humanness. But marriage is different that way. It is like moving from playing American football on the street with your friends where two-hand touch is all you need to have tackled the person to full-on contact with helmet and pads and people running full speed into you. Parts of your body that you didn't know could hurt begin to feel sore. But where you allow love to cover, you can acknowledge your faults, understand that both of you are accountable, and seek help from marriage counselors, roofers, well-diggers, and the best structural engineers you can find for the promotion of your spiritual, emotional, and physical lovemaking relationship.

People, Places, & Things

While most conversations about fidelity center around people, we cannot turn a blind eye to the seriousness of places and things. Infidelity with people, places and things occurs when either spouse invests more time and energy into anything outside of their marriage (with the exception of one's spiritual growth). I often sought the affection of other women because I viewed my wife at the time as being interested in other things except for the marriage (Note: two wrongs don't make a right). We were both unfaithful to our marriage. Within five months of being married, a conversation with my wife at the time about priorities and life goals revealed that the marriage was not her number one priority. She clearly stated that the marriage should be my first priority, but the marriage for her fell into fourth place behind furthering her education, furthering her career, and skincare. And as she said is as she did. For more than half of the time married, she pursued her academic and career goals. Meanwhile, I clamored and begged for her attention.

If you can recall, earlier in the book I mentioned how I sat on the edge of the couch after a year of marriage crying and asking my wife at the time "Why don't you make love to me?" "Why don't you pay me any attention?" and "What's wrong with me?" This was the case for much of the marriage. Adultery was being committed with places and things.

Your role as a husband is to reasonably meet the spiritual, emotional, and physical needs of your wife. While everything is not cut and dried, there needs to be a safe space for communication and transparency prior and during the marriage that allows for these needs to be met. Unfortunately, the circumstances of her or your life and career goals may place either of you between a rock and hard place of meeting each other's demands. But if you are married without the marriage as your first priority, then you cannot meet the spiritual, emotional, and physical needs of your spouse. You are committing infidelity with whom or what you are spiritually, emotionally, and physically meeting the need of, which includes yourself. These issues reveal themselves through long hours on the job, constant pursuit of certifications, consistently going out with friends and colleagues, fulfilling obligations to your church or professional organizations, entrepreneurial pursuits, and many more things that clearly backburners your spouse and family. By default, something will always be the center of your attention and motivation. The question is what will it be? This does not ignore joint pursuits or agreed-upon goals. The difference is found in your disposition of heart toward the goal and your spouse.

Time & Timing

Time is the most valuable asset in your marriage and what you spend it doing and with whom you spend it is of paramount importance. **Time** purchases **Moments** and **Moments** accrue **Connections** [Moments/Time=Connections). Time with your wife buys her fond memories and shared experiences that grow the connectivity within the physical, emotional, and spiritual space the two of you have created. If you don't use the time to purchase these moments, then you run the risk of not connecting with your spouse on multiple planes. The connection between partners in a marriage emboldens the bond, strengthens the relationship, and deepens the understanding between the two of you. In other words, you have to take the time to continue getting to know your wife and vice versa well after the ink has dried on the marriage certificate.

What's often misleading is a spouse's ambition/goal/desire being miscategorized as an intention for the betterment of the family. In many cases, these personal goals are just that, personal goals for personal satisfaction. Nothing is wrong with having and pursuing your goals. But the pursuit of these goals comes at a cost; you always take time to give time to something else and can't always make time or make time up for other things. Time spent pursuing other goals can easily result in years of accrued personal fulfillment with little to no depth of trust, honor, and respect to show for in the marriage. You can easily be married for ten years and never really know the person to whom you are married. Spending time to buy moments and accrue connections requires submission and willingness from both husband and wife to being together and growing together. An effective use of spending time together is planning, mapping, and preparing for the times when your time will become split.

I recall going through a financial rough patch when my son and daughter were only three and one years old. I decided to take on a second job in addition to my full-time job. I shared my plans with my father, who in turn told me a story about the wife of a couple he knew who spent much of her time working a second job to supplement the family's income. She did this for years as her children were growing up. It came back up in general conversation one day when the children were adults. The children made it known to the mother how unappreciative they were of the little bit of time she had spent with them while growing up. We all understand this happens in life. To feed your family you need money. But to raise a family or marriage you need time. Time purchases moments and moments accrue connections. They grew up with their mother, but felt very little connection with her.

Think of your marriage as a bank account. The more you deposit into the shared experience of your marriage is the more funds you accrue. Now, as you spend time pursuing other goals, you leave your spouse with moments from which to withdraw in your absence. But if you leave her with a low balance and choose to spend your time elsewhere, you put her physical, emotional, and spiritual needs at risk. Quite often, to fill the empty bank account, in other words, the void or the time, the other spouse may pick up a person, place, or thing to do. They begin to create moments and connections with other people, places, and things which might begin to dilute the physical, emotional, and spiritual space you share in your marriage. And quickly and easily, the two of you can become passing ships in the night. Timing is everything.

SEX MIGHT JUST BE FOR HER

Have you ever considered that the overall presentation of men as the dominant sexual creature may be false? Have you ever considered the notion that men are visually stimulated and more sexually assertive may be a matter of socialization and normalizing practices? One thing we know for sure is that women are sexual and think about sex as much as men do. But societies across the world shun and repress women's sexual inhibitions and create diverging social norms for men and women. However, your wife's body was clearly designed to receive pleasure and arguably receive pleasure more abundantly than a man's body. This in no way means that a man does not receive deep pleasure during sex. However, when considering the challenges a woman's body endures, including their menstrual cycle, pregnancy, and giving birth, their biological design to receive more pleasure during sex may be the balance between the sexes.

I offer this hypothesis on the male-female anatomy to encourage your perspective on sex in marriage to be a dutiful role that supports and explores pleasure for your wife. The mathematical design of sexual pleasure is that giving is receiving, a built-in reciprocal process. The sexual relationship between you and your wife is also a matter of provision for sustaining the marriage. Lovemaking encourages and supports your spiritual, emotional, and physical growth as a couple.

MONEY IN MARRIAGE

CHAPTER 11

After having to resign from my job due to my wrongful behavior, my wife at the time became extremely emasculating, frequently reminding me that she was the breadwinner and the one paying the bills. One day, she stated to me, "I never married a man to take care of him." After eight years of marriage, during which I had a higher salary than her, had worked extra to cover bills, used my credit to finance items for our home, I suddenly found myself categorized by her as being less of a man because I was not working. While waiting for my career to get back on track, I threw my hands at some entrepreneurial ventures. After being the breadwinner for the overwhelming part of my marriage at the time, in addition to my enormous contributions to her academics, the household, and assuming the bulk of the responsibility with the children, it all suddenly had no merit. I had even weathered the financial burden during the times she had been terminated and laid off from work, twice. Nonetheless, she felt licensed to further dominate the marriage at the time due to her high paying salary. Even during the divorce process, she reminded me of things she'd paid for in the previous year.

During this period of not working, the most captivating moment regarding money came when my wife at the time and I met with a church leader to discuss some of our marital challenges, one of them being my unemployment. The church leader urged me to go get a job. I told them I was looking and had been putting in applications. They responded forcefully, "Go work." I repeated myself again. "I'm looking and putting in applications." They replied, "Go get a job." I repeated myself again. They replied, "Any job." I queried, "Just go get any job?" They said, "Yes, any job."

I was startled by the comment, "Any job." "This can't be right," I thought to myself. My wife at the time agreed with the church leader and later asked, "Why did it have to take the church leader telling you for you to understand that?" They had agreed it was better, by virtue of simply being a penis holder of society, that I simply work, "any job."

Understand this clearly: I have never felt above doing any work. But at this moment in time, my wife's salary had more than doubled after receiving her master's degree. Her income was now the sum of both of our previous incomes combined. She made enough money to sustain the very same lifestyle we had. In the meantime, I continued to look for full-time work and take on entrepreneurial projects. The command to get "any job" was not about the monetary reality, but optics. It was about the social normative expectations of a man. Mind you, had it been the other way around, it would have been 100 percent, with all absoluteness, unequivocally beyond a shadow of doubt, acceptable. In fact, it would have been ideal. My wife at the time would have been given complete freedom to "find herself," renew her goals, and transition as I upheld the financials of the household.

Why, as a man, would I not be afforded the same opportunity to emotionally recoup? Get "any job" overrode any emotions I had; simply put, work. My mental health, need for encouragement, and need for emotional support was overridden by a social norm of gender roles that said women emote, men work. Even if I would have earned less a week than the cost of daycare for our children, it was more reasonable to that church leader that I get "any job" than to be a man without a job. Our financial reality was not the problem. The weight of the circumstances seemed heavier at the time than they actually were, but gender roles defeated our reality. Imagine if I had said I didn't marry a woman to take care of her.

This situation caused deep reflection and prayer about our social construct. As I meditated, divine revelation came. Coupled with my training in conflict resolution, I began to see more clearly the lines of division and underhandedness of gender roles and how they actually go against the very Christian-laden values many people claim to have. I observed the deceitfulness of male hegemony and the backchannelled power of women. Ultimately, the ways in which our society promotes money, power, and respect are contentious avenues that hinge on social norms and gender roles, which in reality, keep the poor poor and make the rich richer.

MONEY, POWER, RESPECT

Marriage is appropriately seen as oneness, the merging of two lives into one family of shared resources and support. However, marriages often seem to be one until it comes to the money. Many socializing idioms about marriage, albeit satirical, are based in a certain level of truth. Two in particular come to mind: "My money is her money. Her money is her money" and "Happy wife. Happy life." These two statements speak volumes to the perceived equitability of money and gender roles in relationships. Somehow in the midst of vows and pledges to trust, honor, and have for better or worse and 'till death do you part, the oneness shared in the lives of married couples are easily challenged by who commands a larger income.

Finances can be used as an emasculating weapon in marriages, but why not? Between our religious views on the role of a man, emphasis on individualism, capitalism, and social pressures to appear financially well off, you can easily find yourself undermined after you have made yourself vulnerable to those societal expectations.

The social construct of patriarchy links money to the perception of manhood and power, and in turn, plays a major role in marriages. Money may play an even larger role in the dating process while trying to find a spouse. The constant debates on social media regarding the matter of money and the role of a man usually concludes: the man is supposed to be the breadwinner making enough money to cover most or ideally, all of the bills; it is a woman's choice to work but it is the man's responsibility to be the provider (said to be written in the Bible); and the woman's money is extra money for her to do with as she pleases. These rote responses are usually steeped in patriarchy and backchannels power to women as discussed in previous chapters.

The perspective of the man as head of household and the breadwinner is antiquated rhetoric of a 1950s trope, unfounded for the average American household income in the 21ST century. It is not biblically supported, as I have dissected in previous chapters, and it is a misrepresentation of the historical shifts that have occurred for women over the past hundred years. It is important for you to know this information because 1) you may be trying to live up to false expectations, 2) you may be making financial decisions using unrelated or outdated information, and most importantly 3) you may hold your income and ability to "provide" as core to your identity as a man, which makes you vulnerable to women who may think the same way.

First, there's nothing wrong if you believe your wife should stay at home and you should be the sole financial provider. However, if your reasoning were based on biblical principles, I would maintain that such religious dogma is unfounded as outlined in the previous chapters. Second, the conversation is moot for a man who makes enough money to take care of his family and chooses to manage his household accordingly. Lastly, the conversation is further moot for the woman willing to not work and accept her lifestyle commensurate with the salary of her husband. But for those who aren't, let's continue.

HISTORICAL FACTORS

Over the past hundred years, several key factors have reshaped the economics of our society. These factors include moving from the industrial revolution to the information age, World War II, the Vietnam War, higher education, and the National Organization for Women (NOW).

During the North American industrial revolution, the United States of America experienced economic boom through several major industries. Five men are notable for their contributions. Cornelius Vanderbilt and the railroad industry; John D. Rockefeller and the oil industry; Andrew Carnegie and the steel industry; J.P. Morgan and the power industry with General Electric; and Henry Ford and the assembly line of the car industry. These labor-intensive industries were built mostly on the backs of male labor and in many instances child labor. While women were employed in some of these industries, the vast majority of these jobs literally required manpower.

World War II (1939-1945) required women to leave their homes and serve their country. Many of them joined the armed services as nurses, drivers, and clerical assistants. Also, many women left the home to fill the void of men in non-military roles. Women repeated this cycle again in and throughout the United States involvement in the Vietnam War (1965-1973).

During war times, higher education experienced an increase in female attendance and leadership, replacing the male population that had gone off to serve in the armed forces. Higher education institutions experienced a decline in female attendance and leadership after WWII. However, an uptick in female student attendance placed them on a trajectory of outearning men in bachelor's and master's degrees by the mid-70s. Women in higher education has remained on an upswing since.

Instrumental to the efforts of women was the National Organization for Women (NOW). Established in 1966, the NOW organization moved the women's suffrage movement from the late 1800s into another gear as they focused on equality in employment, education, violence against women, and other issues relevant for the advancement of women. Note the overlap of NOW's establishment, the Vietnam War, and the growth of female students in higher education.

Lastly, as we have moved out of the industrial revolution where we saw factories, steel mills, electric companies, and transportation growth through railroads boom, the late 1990s and the 21ST century has brought us into the Information Age. In this age, knowledge is the commodity, not muscles. Women may not have been able to lift steel, brick and mortar to build a bridge, but at the click of a mouse on a computer they can impact organizations and industries. In the Information Age, computers, emotional intelligence, and diversity and inclusion through civil rights are the commodity. Women have had the most flexibility and opportunity to participate in society and be gainfully employed within the Information Age.

However, in spite of these advances, our social conversation in the 21ST century has boxed many women into a rubric from which they have already graduated through the efforts of the Women's Suffrage Movement. I am therefore leery of women who attempt to play both sides of the fence by taking advantage of their advancement while holding men accountable to a time and place from which they have advanced. The 1950s are a long way behind us.

TRUTH SERUM: THE COST OF LIVING IN THE 21ST CENTURY

The average household bills will vary according to region of the country, city, or town. State laws or city laws regarding zoning and taxes will also impact the cost. The neighborhood association and its additional cost such as a homeowner's association fee also impact the costs. The greatest impact on cost of living may be children and the location of your residence.

As our metropolitan/urban centers have densified over the decades, inflation and the significant increases in cost of living, while wages remain the same, is a constant economic reality. Mathematically, that means the vast majority of Americans are earning less each year by retaining the same salary they had the previous years. Not only that, how capital is generated in the 21ST century has shifted with the prevalence of social media and technology.

Real people with real families and real responsibilities statistically require a two-household income. By the time you calculate mortgage/rent, utilities, groceries (have you seen the cost of milk lately?), daycare (kids are extremely expensive), car note, various types of insurance, personal hygiene, beauty expenses, entertainment, and state and local taxes, you have a massive financial responsibility on your hands. It is absolutely amazing for the couple who can afford this on a single salary. However, simply put, the vast majority of people cannot. Our economic and political climate does not allow for it.

The reality is that two-thirds of Americans earn less than $41K annually. Also, more than 50% of married couples are both gainfully employed. Traditional homes, where only the father is gainfully employed, is highest amongst families with children under six years old. The national U.S. Census and Bureau of Labor show that married couples with children who are both gainfully employed earn more money overall, increase their earning potential as they get older, and acquire more assets in the long run. For the average American, the cost of living for a married couple with children older than six years old is not sustainable on the average income of one spouse alone.

Can you get another job in another field? Start a business on the side? Or find other ways to generate residual income? Sure. Absolutely. One of the most underwhelming realities of our society is that industries vary in salary. The accounting graduate starts at $55,000 while the broadcast journalism graduate starts at $35,000. That is nobody's fault. We cannot live our life fueled by money at the expense of our passions. The career services department of colleges and universities and even some high schools provide testing that match your personality to industries. It is not anyone's fault that you may be more communicative as a journalist and have zero passion for mathematical details. Yet, here you go attempting to be an accountant because of the salary. As you see, the political, economic, and the social construct of gender roles will never balance the scales.

THE WARM & FUZZY RHETORIC

We, societally, like the warm fuzzy feeling of *tradition.* However, you don't have to dig deep to realize that we naturally establish social homeostasis in order to balance our lives. Meaning, we probably discuss traditional values more than we practice them because those traditional values of the 1950s are no longer practical in the 21ST century. Social homeostasis occurs through adaptation to new norms, including gender roles, in order to maintain a quality of life, find meaning in our relationships, and balance our family dynamics.

Our financial economy is not the same as in biblical times. Couples with children are further burdened with having to make choices between working and the cost of raising their children at home. I wonder what Apostle Paul would say to the church regarding daycare costs. I wonder what he would say if your wife earned a $150,000 annual salary and you earned a $40,000 annual salary. By virtue of your wife being the woman, should she leave her job and remain home with the children for the first five years of their life? I wonder, should you even be married to a woman making more money than you? What if she started off at $30,000 and over the years received a series of promotions that skyrocketed her into six figures? Should you divorce her considering a woman is now the breadwinner? It's starting to sound silly, right?

How does denominational religion respond to these 21ST century realities versus what Apostle Paul outlines in the Bible? Many church teachings leave couples in disarray over headship and money, especially when the wife generates a larger income. The inherent problem is that money is a point of power that lends itself to control over resources, reinforced by patriarchal biblical teachings—and a lot of conflict erupts from that type of hermeneutics.

Some religious leaders say the woman should stay home and the man should work as many jobs as he needs to in order to provide for the life they want. Describing biblical manhood as strict adherence to the Bible, one religious organization publishes literature saying it's a wife's choice to work but the man's obligation and a man should not pursue his dreams or his calling on the back of his wife being the main financial provider. Considering the American approach to college and career readiness, how can the Church pin down one method of approach across a diverse group of people with different goals and visions for their family? If the wife had a six-figure income and no children, could the man's aspirations for law school not be pursued as a full-time student? How many women have pursued their goals on the financial strength of their husband? But many will selectively say it's different for men than women when it comes to financial matters in relationships. Yes, it WAS before, but not in the 21ST century. Unfortunately, these types of teachings relegate the woman and the man to one respective station in life: the categorical function of a man is to work and the categorical function of a woman is to be in the home. Too much in our society has changed for us to be subjected to that indoctrination. A man's purpose is not to work and a woman's purpose is to not take care of the home. I wonder if the Proverbs 31 woman had a higher income than her husband? You can bypass this adversarial issue by understanding the meta-value that God is your provider. How that manifests will look differently in each household.

PROVIDER & PROTECTOR

In the patriarchal effort to place men as the ruling class, women acquire power through the very same rules established through patriarchy by holding men accountable to those rules. Her power, acquired by holding the man accountable to his very own rules, allows her to define and control the perception of his manhood. Patriarchy has set the rules in play that man is the head of the woman and breadwinner of the home while the woman ought to stay home, commit herself to childrearing and domestic duties without any obligation to gainful employment. She now holds your feet to the fire for rules you were both born into and have never decided for yourself. Women are not weak and have found great equilibrium in defining and shaping the identity of men through these rules.

You are a man because you are a man. Your job is to grow into being and continuously be the best man you can be. Too often, the identity of a man is wrapped up in his *doing*, as opposed to his *being*. You are quickly labeled, emasculated, or effeminized if your behavior does not line up with predetermined tasks that demonstrate masculinity. Whether you pump gas or open doors for her or not does not define your manhood. You are a man because you are. Be chivalrous, be kind and caring, but detach your identity as a man from these rote tasks that you have had no hand in determining for yourself as a measure of your manhood. Recall in previous chapters we discussed God as Jehovah-Jireh, our provider. It is not your job to provide. It is God's. Your role is to be a steward over your marriage and resources.

My path to recovery from unemployment was a long, arduous road. But it was never about the money. If the cattle upon a thousand hills are His (Psalms 50:10), then so is the job and the money. And when mistakes and wrongdoing occur, there is nothing a broken and contrite heart cannot fix (Psalms 51:17). This will never eliminate the judgment and justice that comes with our decisions and actions, but "we know that all things work together for good to them that love God, to them who are called according to His purpose" (Romans 8:28). Be a purpose-driven man that is purposeful with his money as well.

PHYSICAL & EMOTIONAL ABUSES IN THE MARRIAGE

CHAPTER 12

Men are equally emotional beings. However, socialized to quell our emotions, many men reach a boiling point and out spills their emotions in the form of hypermasculinity, depression, violence, or chauvinism. The road to that slippery slope of internal conflict stems from the crisis men are socialized into as they attempt to find their identity. So many cues from so many outlets attempt to inform men and women of who they are. The purveyors of rhetoric are all men and women attempting to control the thinking and acting of other men and women through social norms, religious indoctrination, the news media, and popular culture and entertainment. The same outlets provide women the green light to wrap their identity in a victim mindset and justify their victimization as moral retaliation or in defense of their emotional security. This results in the undercutting of men's emotions to meet a predetermined definition of what a man is supposed to be. Women derive power by holding men accountable to these norms, and when those standards are not met, hold the power to emasculate the man, thereby fracturing his identity. A woman's buy-in to the socially accepted viewpoint that women are largely the underclass and victims of society permits them to knowingly and unknowingly victimize men. For example, as stated before, women can hit men but a "real" man should never strike a woman back. Wives can, no doubt, attempt to control what the identity of her husband looks like. But she is only doing what she has also been socialized to do.

Men frequently experience physical, emotional, and even sexual abuse in marriage. The nature of society to protect women and children, due to their lesser physical strength, easily presents an unbalanced scale that favors women to not be seen as perpetrators, giving women an upper hand with law enforcement. The same logic causes the emotional needs of men to be overlooked, leaving men to endure their battles in silence. And oftentimes, when men reach out to other men, they receive feedback that promotes endurance rather than solutions. It's easy to fall into retaliatory behavior after a woman initiates physical abuse in the relationship. Part of the problem is, again, the perception. Many women don't see their actions as domestic violence because a "real man" doesn't hit a woman.

WOUNDED ANIMALS

a poem

I remember the first argument we had that got physical.
I was scared.
We had just gotten married and the nostalgia hadn't even cleared
And when I think about it more the nostalgia was never really there

The only thing present were two people in a three-bedroom condo
With a square footage smaller than the two-bedroom condo next door
I can only imagine what they could hear next door
We were caged, legally married cats with huge roars

She was not happy about me going out that evening
Truth is, it could have been for a whole 'nother reason
I don't remember, cause when it was that long ago
You don't remember what started the fire
You just remember the burn was slow

That night she raised her voice at me
And the things she had to say left my mental in disarray
Rapid fire, tongue-lashing expletives
About my pastor and what my church is

And other things that had everything to do about nothing
I took steps back as she was coming, my way
Her steps were slow at first, then gradually faster
I felt like prey

I was numbed by her coldness
Taken back by her boldness
To a time when I was nine and felt defeated
By a bully in the same place that I called home for that summer
He made me feel small
I was the fastest kid on the block when playing touch football
And when the game was over he still played 'touch' football
His lies, blatant like nine-months of pregnancy,
To his parents about dishes in the sink grounded me
Anything wrong in the house was blamed on me
Speaking up for myself would only bring more punches to my arm
He would smile and act jokingly
But I knew the storm that came after the calm

And here I am all these years later
Trapped in this Arnold Schwarzenegger movie, Total Recall
And I'm Colin Farrell
A remake for me to retake the same test

And it all came back to me, I was scared
Her hair stood up as she leaned in with her chest
She walked me down till I had nowhere to go
Nothing can prepare you for when your spouse becomes your foe

Backed into a corner I couldn't take the rest, so
In an attempt to calm the storm, I opened my palm
Like a coiled cobra lunging
And I struck her

In that nanosecond of the decision-making process
My SWOT became a swat as I reasoned
She was ***Strong****, I was* ***Weak***
She was not giving me an ***Opportunity*** *to leave*
I felt ***Threatened*** *by her breach*

And she just needed to snap out of it
And in the same breath of her roar
She asked why and what did you slap me for
But I don't think she would have understood how she was
hurting me more

How this three-bedroom condo
Just became another place where I've been maimed
She walked me down, while putting me down
Cornering me with angry defamations to my name

Sometimes the hunter and the prey are really the same
A vicious cycle of behavior you throw away but gets recycled
She was preventing me from going past her
I did not know what more she was after

From issues with her father that pulled us farther
From being the type of couple that makes the marriage go
further
Wounded animals caged together
Go at each other to protect their wounds
How words from broken faucets
Cause stomachaches in our wombs
And she'll remember the slap
And I'll always remember the cage, the corner, and the attack.

I was arrested for domestic violence in the fourth year of our marriage. I distinctly remember the judge chuckling after reading the incident. "I've never seen someone arrested for throwing a pair of pants," said the judge. The state prosecutor replied, "I think it was more so the push, Your Honor." I was wrong for throwing a pair of dress pants and pushing her. About a month later back at our home, after the case was dropped, my wife at the time said, "Maybe if you had called and apologized I wouldn't have called the police." I didn't see calling and apologizing as a road to conflict resolution. I saw it as another means of control to manipulate the relationship.

Looking back, I can see why I was arrested. I was always perceived as the angry Black man while she was always the soft spoken and calm woman not showing any signs of aggression. Seeing her switch up her behavior when the police arrived would further upset me. My wife at the time was physically and verbally abusive from the very beginning of our marriage. However, calling the police was not an option I had considered. Therein lies the major distinction between men and women and the issue of domestic violence. I never considered using the law as a means to protect myself against her.

Domestic violence in our home was a catch-22. For example, she would block the front door to prevent me from leaving our residence when arguments became heated. When trying to move her out the way, she would claim I was putting my hands on her and use that as the basis for her calling the police. On other occasions, when trying to leave our residence to calm down, she would shadow my movements and push me back to prevent me from leaving. She once threw my keys behind the entertainment center and had begun kicking me in the side and stomach as I lay on the carpet trying to retrieve them. To prevent arguments on the phone to spill over to the house, I would leave the condo as she arrived.

On occasions she preemptively parked her vehicle behind mine to prevent me from leaving, in hopes of forcing me back upstairs to re-engage her. Unsolicited, I have had a pot and a remote control thrown at me with force. But I never called the police on her.

Our society tends to more easily empathize with women as victims while sidestepping the very same issues faced by men. It's easy to agree on principles, but people's social perspectives tend to override those principles, especially when it comes to the matter of abuse against men. Domestic violence against a man does not have the same disdain. A woman raping a man nearly sounds unreal. In principle, we can all agree that no one should physically hurt, harm or engage in unwanted physical touch. We can also agree that emotional and sexual abuses are just as unacceptable. But in practice, we hold the genders to different standards.

DOMESTIC VIOLENCE

Material I've read during my conflict resolution studies coursework indicated women were 14 times more likely to commit smaller acts of domestic violence while men were more likely to commit fewer but more violent acts. That's an alarming statistic, but a very important piece of information to note as it places women in the center of domestic violence as perpetrators. Men, as I once did, often overlook these smaller acts of domestic violence because they tend to not carry the power or force that may cause injury. In general, domestic violence is severely underreported by men. Unfortunately, it appears many women disregard their actions as domestic violence because a "real man" does not hit a woman back under any circumstance. This means women who think along these lines believe they are permitted to administer physical abuse, but you are not permitted to retaliate. That socialized thinking is deceptive and further emotionally abuses men as they are told to "man up." Men don't have the luxury of feeling victimized (especially by a woman)--it cuts across the definition of being a man. Subsequently, the socialized definition of being a man includes being able to take and accept the way in which we are abused. Being forced to accept abuse normalizes abuse, leaving many men unaware that they are being abused, and in turn chalk it up to the woman being "a woman."

In spite of all the talk about who is from Mars, and who is from Venus, and who keeps the toilet seat up or down, men and women ultimately want the same thing: to be respected, trustworthy toward each other, and treated honorably. Unfortunately, on many occasions the woman's smaller acts of domestic violence agitate a large act of domestic violence from the man. But again, we have a catch-22 that leaves relationships broken in deep emotional ways. Part of the problem appears to be that men overlook the smaller acts as being domestic violence or outright don't know that they are even experiencing domestic violence or emotional abuse. Many women are prepped to not tolerate a man hitting them. Are men prepped for domestic violence perpetrated against them? Let's examine the following short scenarios:

Scenario 1: During an argument you block the door and prevent her from leaving the room or house because you are determined to address the issue.

> *If she called the police and reported you were not letting her leave the house, the inclination for law enforcement officers would probably be that you are holding her against her will and that may be considered false imprisonment and domestic violence. See how that works?*

If the situation was reversed, you may consider moving her out of the way (as I did) before calling the police. Physically attempting to move her from the door is unwanted touch and could be considered domestic violence. However, her actions to prevent you from leaving the home is false imprisonment for holding you against your will.

The problem men may face is thinking they can handle the situation on their own, which unfortunately may lead to an escalation of the problem. My advice is to de-escalate the situation with words that affirm her feelings, reflect understanding, and propose a solution. But what do you do when your best attempt to verbally communicate does not give you the results you are hoping for? And what do you do if you don't want to acquiesce to her demands and you really want to exit the room, which is your right? After all, she does not have the right to keep you against your will. Even an affectionate touch at this moment may be considered threatening to her. However, you have a right to protect yourself using law enforcement.

Scenario 2: During an argument she jabs her index finger into your chest and concludes her remarks with a final jab to your forehead.

> *Is that physical abuse? Would you call the police and report it? Do you feel threatened or fearful? Are you used to this behavior from her? Does her physicality usually not escalate from this?*

How often do men share with their male friends that they've been physically abused by their wife? How often do these male friends encourage him to protect himself by calling the police? On the other hand, if she called the police after you jammed your index finger into her temple that would be considered domestic violence and grounds for arrest.

Because the woman's smaller acts of physical violence toward him may not hurt or cause serious injury, he tends to ignore the abuse. But his retaliation has a higher potential to do more physical harm to her. And when that happens, the United Nations, Global 8, North American Free Trade Agreement, Black Ops, Naval Seal, The Avengers, Handy Mandy and his cousin, and Superman and Batman cease their duel to respond to the threat of violence against her. Men understand the more extreme situations of abuse, such as a frying pan, hot grits or iron hitting him across the head. But in many instances, even in cases of extreme violence, men are less likely to report physical abuses against them. He may overlook physically harmful acts because the abuse has been normalized, coupled with the social stigmas of being a man.

Your job in domestic disputes is to first and foremost protect yourself. State the obvious, such as, "I'm upset right now and I would like some time to myself to think this over. It's not appropriate for you to block the door and prevent me from leaving." And by all means, call the police.

Why is Western Society More Prone to Side with Women?

Men are stronger. But that is the oxymoron of the situation. Why would a woman be physical with a man knowing he is naturally stronger than her and challenge him to not hit her back? This argument breaks down every time because men don't think in terms of strength. Men think the same way a woman thinks when she is being hit: emotionally. Women tend to raise the bar for men to be mature and rational, which also means that he should know his strength, while she lowers the bar for her to be emotional and physical. As mentioned before, men and women want the same thing and, in many ways, we process our experiences similarly. A man does not physically retaliate because he is thinking about his strength; he retaliates because he is thinking about his feelings. Furthermore, examine how she acquires power through domestic violence committed against the man by holding him accountable to not retaliate according to the rules of masculinity. In so doing, she defines his masculinity as to what is acceptable behavior (not retaliating) while maintaining her position to be physically violent.

Why Are We Generally More Inclined to Protect Women?

Life comes through women. To protect the woman is to protect future life. It is an overarching spiritual and biological sense of responsibility we feel because she is the receptacle, the carrier, and the deliverer of life. We also tend to see women as gentle, kind, caring, and nurturing creatures. However, while men tend to not define themselves as gentle, kind, caring, and nurturing, men exhibit the same attributes. Unfortunately, women are then fed the same misnomer and subsequently categorize men as largely potential brutes, more prone to violence, barbaric, aggressive creatures, when in fact women can be the very same way.

Statistics show 1 in 3 women are domestically abused and 1 in 4 men are domestically abused. That's 33% versus 25%, an eight percent difference. Looking at the general population, clearly women outnumber men, but the difference relative to our topic is not drastic; thirty-three million dollars versus twenty-five million dollars still makes multi-millionaires out of people. In other words, 33% of women and 25% of men still make abusers out of both men AND women.

Hands, Body, and Objects to Self

Men should not hit women; and here's a thought for the 21ST century: women should not hit men. The expectation for letting cooler heads prevail is a matter of maturity, not who is physically stronger. Women cannot expect a man to calculate that he is stronger and could hurt her in the middle of her being physically abusive toward him. When defending one's self, do they think about how much they could hurt the other person or do they think to defend themselves?

I do not support the use of law enforcement as a means to control or to be vicious toward your wife (that's wrong and two wrongs don't make a right). Generally speaking, if you cannot manage your conflict without having law enforcement involved, then you probably should not be married, or you and your wife are in serious need of marital counseling. But know that marital counseling won't fix the problem if you or she are more interested in being right and less interested in actually fixing the problem.

The mistake many couples make is using marital counseling to try and fix the other person instead of developing him or herself. A person cannot and will not address their issues until they are ready or life's circumstances (not you directly) force them to deeply introspect. Nonetheless, men need to know that women can be abusive, recognize the abuse, and know their rights and how to protect themselves against domestic violence. Don't cheat, don't hit, protect yourself.

DIVORCE IN MARRIAGE

CHAPTER 13

Marrying to divorce was never the goal. Yet after the "yes" to the proposal and exchange of vows, so many people find themselves at this crossroad. Mostly because we bring so many deep-rooted, hidden, and unforeseen idiosyncrasies, expectations, and ways of thinking and behaving that slowly but surely work against the relationship. Our best intentions to screen for these potential elements in our mate will always come up short. What's more is that we and our significant other grow and evolve as individuals with our own tastes and uniqueness that has to constantly be negotiated throughout the marriage. And in many instances, people fail to agree.

Marriage is a profound, seemingly bottomless, tying of the spiritual, emotional, and physical properties of who we are that divorce, at the core, especially when children are involved, is like trying to pull apart conjoined twins who share the same heart and brain. Fortunately, or unfortunately, most people are not taught how to go through a divorce proceeding. Learning about the process of divorce usually comes too late. You get a crash course from talking to your attorney, talking to someone who has been through it before, or googling. However, for two reasons divorce is inevitable: 1) we enter marriages in a state of divorce; and 2) there are things that you need to divorce before marriage, or it will divorce you.

STATE OF DIVORCE

Most marriages begin in divorce as most of our single lives were spent reinforcing behaviors that lead to divorce. These behaviors are socialized norms that dictate gender roles, creating expectations that are often not transferable to marriage. Socializing agents may include our religious organization, observation of other marriages (especially of our parents), the media, and popular culture mediums such as music and movies.

Individuals bring their past emotional injuries, point of views, beliefs, expectations, and social identity to the table. Oftentimes, you learn how your spouse will actually react to a particular matter after circumstances demand a response. Overall, men and women are socialized differently, which evolves into differing lenses in how we see and perceive the world. Culture is not defined by groups of people, but by the individual. Each person has his or her own culture. The fact alone that you are male and she is female is a state of diversity that has to be negotiated within your marriage. Also, how men are taught to deal with conflict is also a matter of socialization, placing an imprint on what masculinity looks like. In general, how she experiences the world is not the same as you; your daily experience as a man is different from hers as a woman.

The multiple aspects of what is considered normative male behavior, in addition to personality type, culture, and lived experiences, establishes our individuality. Human beings are simultaneously creatures of habit, which makes them easy to understand, yet multi-faceted, ever-evolving, and convoluted in ways that makes them difficult to decipher. With that said, knowing yourself becomes paramount and primary to knowing your significant other.

THINGS TO DIVORCE

There are things you must divorce before getting married or it might become the cause of your divorce. The divorce I speak of mostly deals with ideas, thoughts, and practices that you need to abandon or grow from. In some instances, it might be your purple-colored couch from college that has sentimental value but no aesthetics. Divorce the couch. It might be a sex, alcohol, or leisure activity that is not conducive to your purpose-driven goals. I cannot be too specific about any of these things because they will look different for each man. For example, some people can hold their liquor while others cannot. Divorcing alcohol might be necessary for the husband or husband-to-be who gets drunk and spews insults at people. In this instance, alcoholism can be the cause of your divorce if you don't divorce it.

THE DIVORCE PROCEEDINGS

Divorce is scary in so many ways. It involves a formal third party who has rights over your person in ways that impacts your time and finances. They also judge between you and your spouse without having any real way of knowing the truth and the depth of your situation. You stand in front of people who do not know your or your spouse's heart or intentions. They only know what they see on paper and what is reflected through your attitude in court. The bad person can look like the good person; the good person can sound like the bad person. You are brokenhearted, emotionally defeated, and involved in a process that you may have put yourself in, but forced to endure as it runs its course. How do you trust the lawyer to do what's best for you? How do you watch an attorney defend your spouse who you feel may have wronged you? They are defending your spouse's rights, but it feels more like they are defending your spouse's character.

The court is ultimately there to represent the kids. And in many more ways, their job tends to side with protecting mothers more than fathers. But that approach is becoming more balanced in the court system of many more states. Nonetheless, children can become the pawns and spouses use whatever they find as an emotional or financial upper hand. (My ex-wife once told me she would take the kids and I wouldn't see them anymore.) Someone has to move out of the residence—usually the man. And where do you lay your head? (I plan to one day start a transitional housing complex for divorcing men along with legal resources and access to social services.) Women tend to believe that it's a man's job to take care of them, and the court has held that way of thinking for eons to the detriment of families. These imbalances can be overcome. But the physical, emotional, and spiritual toll it takes on you is something that life might not have prepared you for.

Divorce proceedings are oftentimes not friendly. Quite often, there is no kumbaya and all of the love is sucked out of the room. A spouse uses the financial power they have to acquire a more reputable attorney than yours. A spouse may use emotional jousts during court that only you can read between the lines of. Too many inside jokes that are no longer funny find their way into the dialogue. These silent jabs can only be overcome by a ruthless determination to not let it get to you. It is a strength you never knew you had to have. You might be surprised at how easy it is for your spouse to move on. Or maybe you're both so over it that you are willing to do anything to walk away. It feels as if it's supposed to be dirty and dragged out while simultaneously praying it doesn't become that.

FATHERING AFTER DIVORCE

Being a father has been my biggest joy. I can sadly but truthfully say I understand why and how men come to abandon or become less involved in their children's lives. My good friend and educator Jennifer Felton makes it simple to understand: A man's loyalty is to his wife, not his children. Considering the emotional, sexual, and domestic abuse I had endured throughout the marriage, I wanted to be as far away as possible from my soon-to-be ex-wife at the time. I started applying for jobs on the West Coast to be on the opposite side of the country. I was willing to pay child support and figure out when I would see my children because seeing my ex-wife was painful.

My saving grace was my father and the therapist I had begun seeing during my divorce process. My father would often implore me to do my best with the children and support them as much as possible. Likewise, my therapist and I had very direct conversations about the potential impact of an absent father. I shared with her how I wanted to escape to the other side of the country, but she always encouraged me to consider them.

I am grateful I remained local and present for my children. Today, I couldn't imagine it any other way, but I am thankful for the understanding gained through the experience. It has made me less judgmental of men in that space because I know it first-hand. The process of divorce can have an immense impact on everyone, including the children and just as important, your state of mind. Nobody wins.

WOMEN AS PANACEA AND VICTIM

CHAPTER 13

Panacea [pan-uh-see-uh]:
an answer or solution for all problems or difficulties: cure all

Victim [vik-tim]:
a person who is deceived or cheated, as by his or her own emotions or ignorance, by the dishonesty of others, or by some impersonal agency

In my experience, I have unfortunately but understandably observed that women tend to filter their life through the lens of victimization to be discussed in the section *I See Angry Women.* It appears women tend to remain in a state of continuously perceiving themselves as emotionally and physically vulnerable (especially in comparison to a man), which enlists the need to always be defensive and on guard. That same mentality also enlists the need for a man to be provider and protector of her emotional and physical well-being. However, violence against men occurs from women in this constant perceived state of their vulnerability. When women adopt this mentally socialized identity as the victim, they respond as the victim. What does the cat that feels backed into a corner do? They scratch and claw their way out. Many women come into relationships feeling backed into a corner long before their significant other ever came into their life; but now he has been mauled. And somehow, she is still the victim and the mandates of being a "real" man make his and her victimization his own fault and responsibility to fix. Many women won't like this commentary because it does two things: 1) more judiciously distributes the problem in destructive relationships between the sexes, which 2) forces women to be accountable at a level they are not used to.

The notion of hierarchy in a relationship is false, but it plays into the woman's favor. Buying into the belief that the man is the head, provider, leader, and protector makes him extremely more accountable for the relationship. Meanwhile, a woman can work as hard as she chooses to counter every point of his "leadership" and very little in our social construct holds her accountable for doing so. Being that his manhood is tied to her validation, he is always at her mercy to be recognized and acknowledged as a man.

Women respond to their perceived victimization in a paradoxical manner. In an effort to hide their vulnerabilities and highlight their assets, they present themselves as simultaneously panacea (perfect) and victim (weak). In weakness, she is emotional, vulnerable, and sensitive, and for those reasons should be treated delicately. In perfection, they are strong, invaluable, and the panacea of society. And for those reasons they should be esteemed.

The social construct informs us how to view and treat women in ways that uphold this paradoxical thinking. To name a few, women ought to be pursued or chased, she is the "good thing" the man finds, she is the fairer sex, and she is the portal through which life comes into this Earth. On the other hand, she is highlighted as emotionally, intellectually, and physically inferior, and oftentimes relegated to domestic duties in concert with the thinking that her emotionality prevents her from leading in more global ways. Overall, she claims to need provision and protection for both sets of reasons, panacea and victim.

In order to overcome these compacted views, her identity evolves to ways that negotiates power and self-preservation. For example, she may use her sexuality to attract attention while rejecting the ways in which she is sexually objectified. She retains the power to sexually exploit herself and reject others from sexually exploiting her. In effect, she is able to use either side of this coin to forward her agenda toward provision and protection.

In this system of duality, panacea (perfection) and victimization (weakness), Westernized women are able to appropriate masculinity in their perfection and conveniently retreat to their femininity in their weakness while also maintaining their femininity as a position of strength. In other words, she retains a level of power when using masculine traits and retains a level of power when she retreats to her feminine traits. In practice, a woman can hit a man (masculine trait of aggression) but a man should never hit a woman back (feminine trait of being weaker and power). She is simultaneously pulling power from both sets of traits. Just imagine the context on its own: only one party can be physically violent toward the other party, and by virtue of who the aggressor is (female), cannot be retaliated against. (Think about trying to defend yourself from police brutality.) She is able to demand being emotional as a position of strength, and for no other reason than on the account of being a woman.

Furthermore, it is the expectation that a woman's state of perfection is automatically accepted by virtue of her simply being female. Beyoncé, pop star and actress, sings the song "Flawless," which exclaims, "I woke up like this." This song, pushed into the social conversation, echoes the sentiments of women as automatically perfected entities (because of their gender). This thought process creates a sense of entitlement for provision and protection because of her worth AND because of her weakness. By virtue of being a female, they believe they should automatically be accepted as perfect, flawless beings that men should aim to win and maintain the affection of through provision and protection. For example, you open doors, pull out chairs, and provide for women for a baseline reason: she is a female. It is expected, considered appropriate, and is therefore an entitlement.

However, women are trapped in this space because the socialization process informs them that marriage is a rite of passage—womanhood is achieved through marriage. As such, the collective thought of women is forced to produce an image of perfection in order to be seen as ideal for marrying.

Meanwhile, the social construct of masculinity does not allow a man the flexibilities of this duality of perfection and weakness, masculinity and femininity. Manhood, for a heterosexual male, is typically seen as always demonstrating masculine traits. But women, on a daily basis, use their image of auto-perfectness to hide their vulnerabilities and demonstrate phenomenal strength in their progressive agenda. They have simply been allowed to be less accountable for their role in relationships. Beyoncé also sings "girls run the world" while James Brown croons "it's a man's world." Which is it?

VICTIMIZATION

I recognize the challenges women have faced in society at large. Their victim mentality did not occur by happenstance. Women have historically been viewed as second-class citizens, paid lower wages than men, and incur more extreme violent offenses against them such as rape, sexual assault, and murder. These historical factors have created the essence of women as victims, by and large throughout most countries. This is not a phenomenon; it did not suddenly happen. Women have been in this place throughout societies for centuries. It is not the natural order. The second-class position of women has been taught and has remained deep within patriarchy and major world religions, including Christianity, Hinduism, Judaism, and Islam.

On the other hand, quite often in today's society, women's lived experiences do not totally concur with the heightened perception of victimization historically connected to women. In other words, they are not directly victimized. Her awareness of the possibility heightens her defensiveness against being a victim. People tend to internalize injustices committed against people, places, or things that reflect their identity. It becomes a moral obligation to fight against the possibility of it happening to you. However, what a person believes they are, so they become.

Our Western society promotes the perception of victimization through branding and marketing, spearheaded by media outlets and major entertainment companies. For instance, the media's reporting paints the Black man as the face of crime. The perception of Black males in America as criminals was hyperbolized by the 1915 silent epic drama *The Birth of a Nation* directed by D.W. Griffith. The imagery from that film greatly impacted policing and the perception of Black men for decades. Also, the reporting of crimes involving Black assailants and Black victims are slanted. The face of poverty is a Black child, albeit there are many poorer white kids using government assistance throughout the United States of America. The face of terrorism is Middle Eastern in spite of white males carrying out more mass murders on American soil than their Middle Eastern counterparts. The face of domestic violence is male even though research on intimate partner violence reveals women are equally and sometimes more domestically violent than men. In short, many people would rather a successful lie than an inconvenient truth.

Similarly, women, who have lived in a world that has religiously, economically, politically, socially, and psychologically subjugated them, will frequently view circumstances as a matter of sexism, colorism, racism, and victimization, even within the marital space. The victimization of women in our larger society (her socio-personal experiences) filters down into her sense of self and her place in society (her intrapersonal relationship), which impacts her relationships with others (interpersonal relationships), including her husband. If her global thinking, influenced through the world at large, has adopted the lenses of victimization, she naturally defends herself and, in the process, may victimize her husband. The unfortunate matter is that men in society are viewed as natural victimizers, thereby making his victimization, if even acknowledged, of second-class importance.

The truth is we are all victims of society at some level or another. It should not be a competition for who is the most deprived. In fact, multiple schools of thought have created hierarchies that either promote the man over the woman or the woman over the man, placing either of them in a potentially dominating role.

In their pursuit for upward mobility, you will find women can be, just like any human being, abusive, domineering, competitive and destructive. In my observation, women have become the new man in that their behavior is increasingly reflective of sustained masculine traits of hegemony. In other words, they equally prioritize amassing power and control. They do this while also capitalizing on the social construct of how women are perceived through their feminine traits. The way we socially discuss the image and role of a woman—often different from what we practice—is to see her as the kinder, gentler, and more vulnerable of the sexes. Because women are marketed and branded as the more vulnerable and fairer of the two sexes, she is provided a loophole that permits her to be domineering while not appearing as such.

The point here is that I can simultaneously acknowledge the victimization of women and the conglomerate of victimization across multiple groups of people, including men. If we can understand that various groups of people have their own story of victimization, then it's my hope that we can understand the conflict that occurs when various degrees of victims interact with each other, all vying for acknowledgement and validation. I see angry people across the divides of race, nationalism, and gender roles. These hotbeds of conflict are largely the result of failed expectations in our society. If we can understand that others are reasonably angry, and why they are angry, then maybe we can have greater understanding and empathy toward our mates.

I See Angry People

In the United States of America, the economic strata are found in access to higher education, earning potential, and capitalism. The psychological expectation is wrapped in the message of life, liberty, the pursuit of happiness, and justice for all. There is a peace of mind that comes with having a piece of the American pie, your own house with a white picket fence. The political expectation provides no taxation without representation, voting rights with votes that count, and political leaders who faithfully and rightfully execute the law in the people's best interest. The religious expectation is the right to practice your personal faith to a God who favors you in your pursuit of life, happiness, liberty, and justice through good works, faith, and tithing. The social expectation is acceptance throughout society in spite of our gender, race, sexual orientation, physical and mental abilities; it is the freedom to express ourselves without ridicule or being demonized.

The incredible truth is that very few people actually get to *catch* the "happiness" as described by the American dream. The American dream is a pursuit intended to have people in continuous hunt of the carrot that dangles under the name of life, the pursuit of happiness, liberty and justice for all, a democratic government, and capitalism. The economic, psychological, political, religious, and social promise of many societies seems to escape the grasp of citizens because it leaves them in a state of sustained pursuit. The dissatisfaction from the continuous evasiveness of actualizing the expectations of happiness has created sustained anger in people. I see angry people.

Angry White Men

Michael Kimmel's *Angry White Men: American Masculinity at the End of an Era* describes the "aggrieved entitlement" of white American men who feel they have been duped out of the American dream because of affirmative action and the influx of immigrants. Kimmel points out the historical privilege of white men and their economic advantage above women and people of color. Kimmel explains the anger of white men who see themselves entitled to the American dream based on their notion of doing it the right American way. However, when there is no reward of upward mobility, there is a feeling of humiliation and a commitment to blame somebody else. Kimmel contends that men's adherence to traditional ideals of masculinity have left many white men feeling entitled to the American dream. And when it does not matriculate, white men are left feeling cheated, unhappy, and unfulfilled. Kimmel refers to their anger as deeply gendered, pointing out that these men are relying on traditional notions of manhood: physical strength, self-control, power. As depicted by Kimmel, I see angry white men.

Angry Black Men

Black men are in the crosshair of the racial and gender divides. The racial divide is the institutional forces confronted on a daily basis; the gender divide are the marital norms experienced in the home (for the sake of this book). The Black man's interaction with law enforcement is particularly stark. The initiative to pour drugs into Black communities across America resulting in arrests and mass incarceration was a plight endured by thousands of Black men. In spite of the statistical fact that white people access and use illegal drugs more than Blacks, it was an irrelevant statistic when it came to stop and frisk. Access to a fair trial with a jury of your peers is as absent as Prince Charming is for women. The killing of unarmed Black boys and men, the publicized narrative of Black men as deviant, criminally minded beings, and the fear mongering over the physique of Black men is deeply ingrained in the psyche of white Americans. Black women face a similar plight as well.

Moreover, as we have moved into the 21ST century, Black Girl Magic has been a resounding marketing campaign for the uplifting of Black women. Meanwhile, Black men are more frequently met with Black Man Tragic at the hands of law enforcement officers and other Black men. The promise of equality, access, liberty, and justice for all seems more evasive to Blacks than any other group when considering the free labor of slavery upon which the United States of America was built.

Along the racial divide, you also have the anger of Black Americans who have been promised the benefits of the Civil Rights Act of 1964, affirmative action of 1961, Fair Housing Act of 1968, and school integration through the landmark case of Brown vs. Board of Education in 1954. Black Americans have not seen heartfelt service from the American government or their white counterparts in upholding the promise of inclusion. The high incarceration rates of Blacks, redlining, socioeconomic cycle of poor neighborhoods, unfunded schools, fewer job opportunities, and the institutionalized modus operandi of racism have resulted in an obfuscated economic, psychological, political, religious, and social world. The promised racial equity for Black Americans has yet to be achieved. I see angry Black men.

Angry Immigrants

People migrate from everywhere to America to plant their foot in the American dream. My father migrated to America in the 1980s and worked his way into citizenship, higher education, homeownership, and entrepreneurialism. This is certainly the ideal that fuels many immigrants—the promise of freedom, capitalism, and opportunity. However, immigrants, especially those from Mexico and the Arab countries, have found themselves at the center of blame for the economic and political climate of many of the proceedings in America. They have found themselves blamed as the cause for job loss in certain sectors. The job loss created economic hardship for many white Americans. They have also found laws pitted against their access to the country, deportation, and separation from their families. Immigrants have also endured the negative perception put forth by political leaders who over-generalize and monolithically group their existence in the United States of America as criminals, rapists, and terrorists. Immigrants have found an obfuscation of the economic, psychological, political, religious, and social American dream on which they had firmly hoped to build a new future. I see angry immigrants.

Angry Women & Wives

Women have been promised protection and provision as part of the economic, psychological, political, religious, and social contract of most societies. Women have been promised chivalry, a contributing father to their children, a knowledgeable leader amongst men, and spiritual leaders for the fulfillment of their lives. But in many instances, women have not found this social contract upheld by men and society at large. The woman's suffrage movement dates back to the story of Adam and Eve when Adam failed to uphold his responsibility toward Eve. Even then, Eve had to negotiate her voice and worth in the society of the Garden of Eden. And women have had to do so for centuries. Not all attempts by women have been warranted, including Eve's, as her pursuit for acknowledgement, according to the story, was ill advised (she was dec'EVE'd). But I see Eve's persistence for acknowledgement and validation as indicative of a larger, more systemic issue of oppression (or silence) that women have historically faced. Women have been physically dominated, viewed as sexual objects, treated as physically weaker, deemed emotionally susceptible, denounced as not intelligent enough to process high-stake matters of business and politics, and physically inadequate for sports. (Note: I am not accusing Adam of seeing Eve as any of the above mentioned.) Women experience far more extreme violence in intimate partner violence, which often enough results in death. The Disney-promised Prince Charming and happily-ever-afters are a far cry from the reality many women have experienced. It is only as recent as 2017 that women in Saudi Arabia4 were given the legal green light to drive. As a driver, she is a leader of sorts, transporting the direction of herself and others. God forbid she transports the minds of the country. It's as if viewing women as leaders outside of domestic household duties is a far-fetched idea for many people.

The lack of a robust healthcare policy for pregnant women and family leave from work to care for their newborn in corporate America is another glaring example of how women are mistreated in our society. Religious teachings on the viewpoints of women have trained us to corporately, politically, and socially view women as second-class citizens. Our society at large, in other words, men, have obfuscated its responsibility toward women, leaving them economically, psychologically, politically, religiously, and socially vulnerable. I see angry women.

Angry Husbands

Most mainstream religions directly or indirectly prepare men to have certain expectations within marriage, upholding a resounding message of patriarchy: the man as the head of the household; the man as ordained ruler over the woman; and the man as empowered through the law of primacy in God's creation of man and woman. Through these religious underpinnings and social constructs, men

4 https://www.nytimes.com/2017/09/26/world/middleeast/saudi-arabia-women-drive.html

grow to expect an accompanying level of submission, respect, and prestige from their wife.

However, many men in the sanctimonious space of marriage discover a dicey situation that challenges their patriarchal view of headship, leadership, and what ruling over the woman is actually like. Men discover that the social contract of headship, leadership, and provider and protector in many instances is a one-way street of conforming to her desires and her definition of manhood and masculinity. They find women to be strong-headed, argumentative, and caught in an ongoing debate regarding the expectations of what submission should look like. Additionally, women/wives present themselves as perfected beings while the man needs to continuously develop and evolve for the expressed purpose of continuously meeting her needs. This context is supported through the notions of her as the emotionally and physically weaker mate. However, while presenting herself as weak, she simultaneously presents herself as the sum total of relationship correctness by virtue of being a woman. Areas in which she falls short should be attributed to her weakness and therefore becomes the responsibility of the man to make accommodations. Yet, in her perceived perfection, women also claim they are the smarter gender and should be recognized for their insight on issues. Many men find themselves subjugated to acknowledging their wife as the entity who really "wears the pants" in the relationship and find themselves captive to the "happy wife, happy life" dogma. Summarily, there is a power struggle in the marriage for control that men thought were originally given to them by virtue of their headship.

Men discover certain realities along the way throughout their marriage: wives have an equal propensity to engage in extramarital affairs; wives can be combative, hostile, and aggressive in ways that are domestically violent toward him (more often through smaller acts of violence); and wives silently protests against the notion of submission. Her protest is a defense mechanism toward the possibility of him "failing" her, which in effect can be a self-fulfilling prophecy. What's more is, according to marital social norms, men shoulder the burden of ensuring a successful marriage arguably more so than women. Again, he has to ensure a happy wife in order to procure a happy life. His happiness is secondary to hers. In practice, it is not true that the weight of the marriage is mostly on the man, but the social normative expectation enlarges the perception of the man as the more accountable party for marital success (similar to how the social norm also enlarges the perception of women as victims).

The court system in some states has updated legislation that balances the legal field for men. For instance, in Florida, custody of a child is automatically awarded 50/50 to both parents when going through divorce proceedings. However, the appeal to women as caretaker and man as provider is still an engrained mentality that steers the rulings of legal matters unfavorably for many men. The family court system has traditionally favored women in matters of child custody and child support. Even in situations where the man is proven to not be the biological father, he is still held financially responsible for the child with no consequence to the woman for perjury. Rape or sexual allegations ruin the lives of many men who are falsely accused. Yet we push the notion that men are sexual beings while somehow neglecting that women are too, which, in a way, rendering a verdict against many men long before they ever entered a courtroom. The only thing needed was a woman to make an accusation.

Men who commit acts of sexual violence deserve to be pointed out and prosecuted. At the same time, the loophole against men in our judicial system is a serious slippery slope that injures men who are falsely accused as much as it injures the women who are actual victims.

Furthermore, many men in their best effort to be an upstanding husband have become overwhelmed by the pressures of wife, family, career, and community activities. With the added caveat of not being able to emote, because it is not manly to vent our frustration, the emotional development of men is stymied amidst the mandate to lead and be the heads of the family. Being the publicly declared head of the household can be a far cry from what actually takes place in the relationship. When you combine the outside world to the duress a marriage might undertake, you find many men who feel they have been left unprotected. As such, I see angry husbands who feel economically, psychologically, politically, spiritually, and socially disadvantaged in much of the American society, both inside and outside the home.

As you see, there is enough evidence for any party to make a case for their anger. Even children have been failed. They have to struggle with an ever-increasing world that has overexposed them to liberalism and tolerance. Children fight attention deficit disorders, depression, confusion about their sexual orientation and gender, socio-economically challenged homes, and school systems that may not adequately teach them. I see angry children all the time. Notwithstanding, where we have a right to be angry, we also have a right to change our perspectives and the way we socialize our environments to positively revolutionize our relationships.

THE LOCOMOTION OF WOMEN

The locomotion of mankind has made triumphant achievements over the course of centuries. Migration with animals has always been the norm, but was restrictive and arduous. Boats have been around for centuries; however, their requirement for manpower and lack of speed made for extremely long voyages. The original cars went no faster than 40 mph. The advent of the steam train helped to place people in contact with one another across great distances in a shorter period of time.

Today, cars speed at 140 mph, the airplane is the safest way to travel, jets can break the sound barrier up to five times, and everyone is a phone call or email away (as opposed to smoke signals and Morse Code). Everything around us has changed, including the way we travel, learn, communicate, think, and even eat. Why then are we so committed to keeping marriages the traditional status quo, retracing faded and outdated lines of division of labor and gender roles, an approach that has usually placed men and women in a subjugated posture?

The greatest change has occurred amongst women. Marriages today must recognize the evident change in female behavior parallel to the evolution of the Information Age. The assembly line was the most popular and widely used process for production during the Industrial Revolution. One person stationed at one location performed one task. Upon completion it was placed on the conveyor belt to move to the next step in the process.

The Industrial Revolution operated under a mechanistic approach, a machine. Employees were not expected to think; the leadership implications were command and control; and the management approach was focused on production and economies of scale. No value was placed on the employees—they were replaceable; employees had no medium for input; and subsequently, employees were never able to fully understand how their role impacted the big picture.

The persistent growth of technology has launched us into the Information Age. Today, businesses consider themselves natural and organismic enterprises. They focus on adaptation and continuous improvement in personnel and technology. Their leadership implications include articulating a vision and attempting to manage under a unity of purpose. The Information Age has placed value on its employees, channels of communication to allow for greater input, and various levels to echo how the role of each impacts the whole.

Women today are products of the Information Age. They are educated and equal contributors to the family income. And while the income levels may vary, their allocation of time to work is equivalent. World War II started a paradigm shift by pushing women into the job market. Vietnam solidified the shift. During and following the wars, many females found themselves working to provide for their home. Soldiers came back wounded and skill-less. Also, many women began pursuing degrees of higher education during this time period. While men were still labeled the breadwinner because of their traditional role (and certain levels of expectation), the practicality of the notion has been challenged and has been changing for more than 50 years.

THE BALANCE

Women cannot play both sides of the gender role game to ensure their access to upward mobility while neglecting or absolving themselves of the responsibilities that come with it. Women who appropriate masculinity contribute to the destruction of marriages and romantic relationships overall. Men, likewise, cannot continue to dominate women through their financial and physical means of power. **Conflicts in relationships arise through the hegemonic approaches of men confronted with the hegemonic approaches of women.** Many men learn a hard lesson when they come to find out, in spite of all the biblical teachings of leadership and headship bestowed to a man, a woman has her own set of advantages that empowers her equally to a man in a romantic relationship.

Women have an amazing opportunity in the 21ST century to level the playing field and make political, economic, and social gains like never before. However, before that can properly take place, the attitude of both men and women in how they see each other must develop past archaic, traditional values of power, dominance, and victimization. Mentor, friend, and colleague David Cole wrote the following in response to a Facebook post I had written:

> *Our entire society is still built around gendered expectations. Girls are taught to be pleasing to others. Boys are taught to master their domain. Girls' play is predicated on communication and relationships; boys on competition and self-mastery. Girls are objectified as things to be admired, possessed, protected and provided for. Boys are taught to possess, protect and provide. Our primal stories reinforce this. The woman's happy ending is usually marriage in our fairy tales, while the boy slays dragons, unites nations and saves worlds. Even the modern dreck in our media frames women as "Real Housewives" even if their lives and accomplishments outside of their man is more evident. Women are told this: You aren't really somebody unless you're SOMEBODY'S somebody: Wife, mother, daughter, etc. We tell boys: "You are what you do/have." Even most of our Abrahamic faith experiences push it. Even though many on this thread may have different experiences, that doesn't negate the fact that our society still is running that program.*

In order for men (and the women who have bought into this way of thinking) to rid themselves of their hegemonic principles, they must exercise curiosity in how they scrutinize the underpinnings of biblical text and revisit how they understand the spiritual intent, time, place, and relevance of gender-infused Scripture. The apostles are not greater than the right-now word of God.

DRESS IT & KEEP IT: WHAT ROLE DOES THE BIBLE PLAY IN MARRIAGES?

CHAPTER 15

Religious texts such as the Bible are deeply entrenched into societies because they provide a moral compass for believers. They also serve as the basis for legislation, social norms, and gender roles. As such, it's important to continue deconstructing and clarifying Scriptures that contribute to the expectations of men and women in marriage. Let's begin with understanding the curse passed on to Adam and Eve and its undoing through the death, burial, resurrection, and ascension of Jesus Christ.

IN THE CURSE VS. OUT OF THE CURSE

Genesis 3 discusses the transition of Adam and Eve out of the Garden of Eden after they disobeyed God's commandment to not eat from the tree of the knowledge of good and evil. Curses, or punishments, were doled out for their actions. God stated the following for Eve: the desire toward her husband, ruled by her husband, and the pain of childbirth. The following were stated for Adam: the tilling of a cursed ground. However, Jesus Christ came on to the scene thousands of years later to redeem mankind back unto God, in effect removing the curse (2 Corinthians 5:17-21). Jesus is referred to as the second Adam (1 Corinthians 15:45-48).

The curse has been removed and we are new creatures through Christ Jesus. Therefore, our efforts for marital relationships should not be focused on natural things; rather, we should understand the opportunity we have as spiritual beings. While our Earthbound bodies have limitations, in Christ, in whom we are neither male or female, we have an opportunity to have a marriage that is out of the curse. This does not start or stop at marriage. Our first relationship, which is with self, must also be out of the curse. The paradigm of gender roles is largely based on the cursed mandates of God, not the redemptive death, burial, resurrection, and ascension of Jesus Christ.

KING LEMUEL'S MOTHER VS. APOSTLE PAUL

Examine the contrast between Proverbs 31 versus the heavily used words of Apostle Paul to define a women's role. Proverbs 31 is the recount of lessons taught to King Lemuel by his mother. In Proverbs 31:10-11 she asks, "who can find a virtuous woman? for her price is far above rubies. The heart of her husband doth safely trust in her, so that he shall have no need of spoil." King Lemuel's mother paints the picture of a motivated woman who is entrepreneurial, industrious, and a contributing provider to her husband, employees, and the community throughout the remainder of the chapter.

On the other hand, Apostle Paul is very clear about the role of women as found in Titus 2:5, which implores women to practice discretion and obedience to their husband, and 1 Corinthians 14:34-35, which states a woman should not speak in church and defer their questions to their husband.

Titus 2:4-5:

> That they may teach the young women to be sober, to love their husbands, to love their children, to be discreet, chaste, keepers at home, good, obedient to their own husbands, that the word of God be not blasphemed.

1 Corinthians 14:34-35

> Let your women keep silence in the churches: for it is not permitted unto them to speak; but they are commanded to be under obedience, as also saith the law. And if they will learn any thing, let them ask their husbands at home: for it is a shame for women to speak in the church.

These Scriptures relegate women to the home and set the stage for a hierarchical framework of headship and submission. The deal is sealed in 1 Corinthians 11:3 and Ephesians 5:22-31, used to establish Christ as the head of the husband and the husband as the head of the wife.

We clearly see how the self-defined role and expectation of women from the words of a woman (King Lemuel's mother) contrasts greatly with the expectations of women from the words of a man (Apostle Paul). But again, it's important to remember that Paul's words are prescriptive to a specific place, time, and problem. The genius in Apostle Paul's ministry is how God used him to write directly to the needs of a particular church. Unfortunately, religion has bastardized Apostle Paul's ministry to establish his recommendations for spiritual governance as infinite law. Knowing the difference between laws, statutes, commandments, and wisdom can greatly broaden your understanding when reading Scripture. I like the way my good friend educator and entrepreneur Yukia Johnson breaks down how to read Scripture, outlining the differences between laws, statutes, and commandments:

> *Laws are set by the nature of our world. They include no directives; they just exist, for example: gravity, the water cycle (precipitation, condensation, and evaporation), and the moon and the tide.*
>
> *Statutes are rules for governing and managing day-to-day. They are often based on environment and circumstances. They are also negotiable and evolving. We usually interchange law and statues (as a form of law). But for this purpose, view statutes as legal regulation codified by a governing entity. For example, consider food regulations and health concerns that are relevant based on the length of time and ability to keep foods from spoiling. Now with refrigeration, and the advancement of preservation technology, regulations have changed accordingly.*
>
> *Commandments are specific instructions given to an indi-*

vidual or specific group of people. For example, in the Bible the following commandments were given (albeit they were not always referred to as a commandment): Samson, don't cut your hair; Abraham, don't marry that race; Abraham, take the lad for sacrifice; Daniel, don't eat their food; Moses, strike the rock. To repeat the commandment won't necessarily give the same results. Moses was told to speak to the rock the second time, not strike the rock. A commandment may not be necessarily fulfilled by another entity, as it's specific to the person or people.

Not following wisdom may not have the same level of consequence of the law, statute, and commandments. However, failure to practice wisdom may cause you to miss out on the efficiency and advantage that they give. For example, consider the book of Proverbs and the letters of Apostle Paul. They are recommendations for living to get the most out of what God intended for us. Laws protect us, statutes govern us, commandments keep us, wisdom blesses us.

BUT I SPEAK CONCERNING CHRIST AND THE CHURCH

Religious denominations, and by that I mean men, have cemented their patriarchal role predominantly through the chapters of 1 Corinthians 11 and Ephesians 5, which outline the hierarchy of Christ, man, and woman.

1 Corinthians 11:3

But I would have you know, that the head of every man is Christ; and the head of the woman is the man; and the head of Christ is God.

Ephesians 5:21

> Submitting yourselves one to another in the fear of God. Wives, submit yourselves unto your own husbands, as unto the Lord. For the husband is the head of the wife, even as Christ is the head of the church: and he is the saviour of the body. Therefore as the church is subject unto Christ, so let the wives be to their own husbands in every thing. Husbands, love your wives, even as Christ also loved the church, and gave himself for it.

Ephesians 5:21-33 states Christ is the head of the husband, who is the head of the wife. It further builds into verse 32, which states, "This is a great mystery: but I speak concerning Christ and the church." As you see, Apostle Paul updated this text to show the hierarchy described in 1 Corinthians 11:3 and later in Ephesians 5:21 was not about the human man and woman, but about God and the church. The marriage between man and woman is symbolic of the marriage between Christ and the Church.

It is documented that the Apostle wrote the books of Corinthians around AD 53-54 and the book of Ephesians around AD 62. Like any good researcher, teacher, or speaker, information gets updated as understanding deepens. Apostle Paul's addition of Ephesians 5:32 is a pivotal turning point in understanding the hierarchy God truly desires to have with his people. The submission of husband and wife is more accurately the submission of mankind (wife) to Christ (husband). This means the human being, male and female, constitutes mankind. The following are key to understanding symbolism in Scripture: 1) the hierarchy is not about husbands being over wives, but Christ being over the church; 2) male and female together establishes the church; 3) male and female are called to be ONE; 4) as one, they (man and woman) submit to their husband in Christ; and lastly, 5) marriage is a natural metaphor of a spiritual relationship

FIND A WIFE, FIND A GOOD THING

The Department of Motor Vehicles does not track how many accidents you avoided, your frequency of travel, your niceness on the road, or your ability to drive with one hand on the steering wheel. Nor does it track road rage, stop signs that were not met with a complete stop, school zones that you drove through at 20 mph, or other smaller infractions. A driver's license is just the starting point of driving. As a matter of fact, the driving test doesn't even expose the teen driver to the highway, a far more intense place to drive. A driver's license says you understand the basics of driving, safety, and you have the prerequisite knowledge to be behind the wheel. A driver's license does not necessarily indicate how good of a driver you are; it simply measures relative competence to operate a vehicle.

A marriage license is similar to a driver's license. The license indicates you now have the right to operate as husband and wife. The license doesn't necessarily indicate just how good of a husband you are or how good of a wife she'll be. Subsequently, to say that when you find a wife you find a good thing is either premature, misleading, or a parable containing a deeper meaning.

Women across many cultures and religions are socialized to see marriage as a rite of passage to womanhood. Added to that is the belief that a wife is the conduit to a husband's greater blessings from God. Proverbs 18:22 (KJV) states, "Whoso findeth a wife findeth a good thing, and obtaineth favour of the Lord." This is VERY true.

When you find a wife, you absolutely find a good thing and that in and of itself is favor from the Lord. What's the catch? The marriage license does not at all mean she's the wife described in this Scripture. James 1:17 states, "Every good gift and every perfect gift is from above."

A "good thing" is a destination. A woman arrives there through deliberate and intentional practices, mentorship, and self-reflection. A woman must learn how to persevere, become self-aware, heal, and learn effective communication, conflict resolution skills, problem-solving skills, money management, time management, and many more things normal to the human experience. Learning how to care, share, love, trust, honor and respect are also important. Men must undergo the very same process in their becoming a "good thing." Nothing about it is automatic.

The conversation regarding women as the conduit of God's favor, or "a good thing," is usually substantiated by the multiplication power of women: man gives a woman a seed, she gives him a child; he gives her groceries, she gives him a meal; he gives her a house, she makes it a home.

However, the discussion surrounding the woman as "a good thing" is often incomplete because it presents the woman as an instantaneous arrival to "a good thing" with no mention of the *how* beyond receiving a marriage license. Some husbands and wives operate their marriage under the influence of divorcing behaviors. That's not a good thing. A woman by virtue of being a woman is not by default a multiplier, the favor, or "a good thing" that a man ought to pursue. The *how* is the process that matures her into "a good thing." Unfortunately, it's often a discussion that usually omits the developmental process it takes to mature into womanhood/manhood and wife/husband.

Moreover, a woman is not more highly favored than a man by default. God is not a respecter of persons (Romans 2:11, KJV). God respects love, joy, peace, longsuffering, gentleness, goodness, faith, meekness, and temperance (Galatians 5:22-23, KJV). The Scripture says against such there is no law. Moreover, the Scripture says there is none good but God the Father (Mark 10:18; Luke 18:19, KJV). A "good thing" can only be of God. And access to God is an equal opportunity process for both men and women.

Between the idea of being a multiplier, favored, "a good thing" and the socialized desire to be in a monogamous relationship, women tend to see themselves as being ready for marriage—and in many instances, readier than a man. They are not ready. In fact, they are just as unprepared as men. A woman's desire for a monogamous relationship doesn't mean she possesses the skills to manage or sustain the relationship. She may not see a need for those skills or not know how to acquire them. Her lack of development is typically not the talking point of her being a "good thing." She, like you, need to have the previously mentioned skills of personal development, a constantly growing level of self-awareness, and the fruits of the Holy Spirit described in Galatians 5 in the process of becoming a "good thing."

DRESS IT AND KEEP IT

God instructed Adam of his responsibilities regarding the Garden of Eden in Genesis 2:15, "to dress it and keep it." Adam was not placed in the Garden to produce, provide, or protect; that was already done by God. He was placed there to be a steward of the resources God had provided. As mentioned before, the story of Adam and Eve is a metaphor of our individual relationship with

God. We have each been given a mandate to dress and keep the Garden of our lives. As our spouse is included in that Garden, your job is to be a steward over her as your resource. She is responsible for doing the same, as you are also her resource to dress and keep.

HOW TO GET AWAY WITH LOVE

CHAPTER 16

Marriage is an ongoing test of the character and integrity of every cornerstone of your life. It tests your presuppositions, your ability to respect, trust, honor, care, share, love, and demonstrate a positive attitude, reflect rightful behaviors, effectively communicate, and maintain the discipline to walk these paths in spite of the social norms and expectations that attempt to lord over your very existence as humans. Ironically enough, you, your spouse, and society at large are often the ones who set up these expectations that springboard into confrontations largely based on our own perceptions and expectations. Furthermore, the merging of two lives is inherently conflicting because you and your wife are different people by nature: you're a man, she's a woman; she experiences a menstrual cycle, you don't; your sex drive, eating habits, sleeping habits, leisure habits, thought processes, political beliefs, religious practices, and level of commitment to various things in life are not exactly the same.

An important dynamic for you to always keep in mind is that up until your point of marriage, you have ALWAYS been single. Your previous girlfriends, series of dating, courting, and shacking were not marriage. The exit strategy serves as a major difference in your past relationships versus your marriage. As boyfriend and girlfriend, living together, you can always leave the relationship relatively penalty free. However, marriage is a ceremonious, spiritual, legal, and contractual covenant that carries legacy, progeny, and rights to your significant other. Many government systems recognize and respect marriage as a point of order. Your marriage license is accepted worldwide. Accordingly, tax laws and healthcare-related laws, amongst other matters, are written for married couples. In short, marriage legally, spiritually, emotionally, physically, and financially binds you together. So, if you were always single prior to marriage, then what has prepared you for marriage? If you have never merged your life with someone else's before, then how do you do it decently and in order? This chapter and the next will provide feedback on some important areas of marriage to assist you to get away with love.

THE FOREST OF FORGIVENESS & THE SEA OF FORGETFULNESS

My wife at the time said it was challenging being married to me because it was hard for me to forgive. She was right. Unknowingly, I had struggled with forgiveness for decades. With the divorce process underway, a conversation with a pastor who had known me my entire life said, "Adrian, even if you're not with her anymore you'll still have a problem with forgiveness." Her words caused great introspection. In a quiet space I began to recall past relationships and my pattern of not forgiving.

The root word of forgive is give, which means forgiveness is a giving process without reservation; giving room, space, and opportunities to the offending party in spite of the offenses you have endured. You give them a chance. You give them the benefit of the doubt. You give them time to recognize their impact and make a change in their attitude and behavior. You give them hope for the possibility of building a better relationship with you. You also give yourself time to reflect, heal, or adjust. Forgiveness, like communication, is a personal culture that has to be established within you first. I am not watering down the offenses people commit against one another. But creating a culture of forgiveness for yourself will greatly prevent you from getting married and doing everything except making it last. There are levels to how deep the dysfunction goes when the marriage begins to break down after years of built-up bitterness and anger. Being a for-you-giver is a prerequisite to getting married and making it last.

In marriage you get to see the worst in each other and see each other at your weakest and most vulnerable moments. You are also witnessing your wife's maturation process as she tackles different emotions and self-discoveries just like you will. The process is more caterpillar than butterfly – it is slow, not so cute, and sometimes uncomfortable. During these times people can say and do some uncanny things.

Feeling trapped in a cycle of constant physical or emotional abuse from your spouse is a hindrance to forgiving. My response to my wife at the time, who every now and then would remind me that I was not very forgiving, was: "Stop doing things to me that I have to forgive you for." But these issues do not happen overnight. As the verbal and physical abuse deepened, then moved into sexual re-abuse and neglect, it became harder and harder to let go of those hurts. I walked around with bitterness while married for at least half of the marriage.

My father was a maintenance supervisor over university and college buildings for nearly 20 years and operated by the mantra: "Fix it before it's broken." The intent of this book was to assist you with fixing it before it's broken. How then do you learn to forgive while in the middle of the storm? The following are important pillars of understanding to adopt:

Forgive Daily. Understand from now that you will consistently (almost weekly) need to forgive your spouse. It's not the major, the-world-is-ending issues that bring this about. It's the small foxes that destroy the vine, especially when you believe something to be important, urgent, or relevant. This plays out in so many ways, including her communication style, time management skills, decision-making process, temperament, level of accountability, what she acknowledges or overlooks, and her overall leadership style. Because sentiments can build up over time, prepare your heart and practice forgiveness starting now. I began practicing forgiveness with everyone, from the bank teller to close business associates in an effort to build up that muscle and establish that culture within my emotional and physical self.

Practice Humanity. Never lose sight of her humanness. I forgot my wife at the time was a human being because I saw her as "my wife." "My wife" speaks to the possessiveness and expectations of roles we have toward our spouses. However, she was a human being and human beings are not perfect, but they can be strong. Notwithstanding, they have moments of weakness, become emotionally drained, overwhelmed by different things requiring their attention, become forgetful, and sometimes drop the ball. Wife and husband experience the world interdependently. Albeit married, each person is still experiencing life, growing, changing, gleaning new revelations, grappling with challenges to their belief system, and navigating uncertainty, fears, concerns, hopes, and dreams. Lower your expectations for perfection. You have to make room for the human being process, which comes with good days and the hope for better days.

Wright or Rong. Removing the need to be right can greatly assist with cultivating a forgiving heart. With no axe to grind or point to prove, you leave your heart open to allowing time to determine the rightness or truthfulness of her or your words. Growth, understanding, and maturation are all time-based and experience-based elements. Let time be on your side in the growing and maturing process of your spouse as well as for yourself. This practice also goes a long way in killing the ego. We sometimes confuse ego with standards. Standards are a set of values and expectations we have for ourselves and others. Ego or humility are the coordinating behaviors that reflect our response to issues that impact these standards and expectations. The culture of effective communication, forgiveness, and finding productive ways to process and respond to what's happening in a particular matter requires patience and humility, not ego.

REGARDING INFIDELITY

Don't Cheat.

COMPATIBILITY VERSUS ATTRACTIVENESS

One of my biggest learning moments was learning to identify the difference between compatibility with a woman versus how physically attractive I found her. I believe looks play a part, but in most instances, it's only an icebreaker, not the main event. In my twenties, I would think I was in-like with her because I found her attractive. My next step would be to try and reorganize my thought process, values, and parts of my personality to try and create a fit. Can you see the problem? I was trying to be someone I wasn't. While my intent was good, attempting to be flexible in order to create a match for her and me, I was making concessions to make a relationship work that otherwise was not compatible.

Compatibility occurs in two phases. Phase one is initial compatibility and phase two is sustained compatibility. In phase one, you may find her personality, humor, intellect, political and religious views, and leisure lifestyle compatible. It's awesome when you find the same things funny and enjoy the same type of entertainment. These initial compatibilities are excellent for jumpstarting the relationship. But they are also surface level matters. Having a mutual liking to the ambiance of a local restaurant, movie genres, and sexual position are not strong enough motivations to sustain a relationship.

As a couple moves into phase two, they are able to identify more sustainable ways of thinking, behaving, and communicating that promote the longevity of the relationship. Your sustained compatibility is culture forming (culture of effective communication and culture of forgiveness) and reveals your deeper, more intrinsic values. Your approach to conflict resolution is largely displayed through your deeper, intrinsic values. Problems and conflicts are inevitable. How you approach problem solving over a period of time more accurately reveals your ability to manage, lead, and be authentic. When assessing your sustained compatibility with her, you are asking questions to yourself such as: *Do I like the way she handles situations when they arrive? Do I like the way she communicates to me and others? Do I like how she manages people in various settings? The homeless? Friends?* Learning if you have sustained compatibility is clarified over time. But you pay attention to it to know if the two of you can get away with love together. Couples, when dating, often spend hours sharing information about their past experiences and future aspirations—all in an effort to project their sustained compatibility.

What does it mean when people say they fell out of love or grew apart? Does that mean you can fall out of compatibility, even when it has been sustained with deeper values over a longer period of time? Certainly, yes you can. Companies that once thrived have found themselves no longer relevant because they failed to evolve. Marriage can incur a similar impact. Compatibility, like the individual, will continue to evolve and deepen over time. But anything worth building requires constant engagement.

KILL THE EGO

The ego can be a venomous personality that goes to great extents to remain active in your life. The ego is often deployed in defense of an insult or emotional injustice we've incurred. The Bible tells us pride comes before destruction (Proverbs 16:18). Pride is a deep determination to dominate, control, and manipulate your spouse for the sake of being right or getting your own way. Oftentimes, it's subtle but reeks of oppression.

Most situations of conflict can be summarily described as a matter of respect. When a person feels disrespected, they feel the need to demand it. People easily feel disrespected when they are not properly acknowledged for their contribution. People expect to be acknowledged in how they are spoken to and treated. People also expect to be acknowledged by acts of appreciation. Respect can be demonstrated as mild as saying thank you or deep as being recognized as employee of the year with your own parking space. Whichever way this plays out for you, because it's a wide spectrum, whenever a person determines they have been disrespected, there is a potential for the supervillain, with its cape on, The Ego, to swoop in to defend their identity and demand acknowledgement.

The ego grows in self-actualization, oftentimes causing mounting negative behaviors that distends into emotional, physical, financial, and sexual abuse. The solution is found in the culture of effective communication, which can only be properly built on a foundation of humility. Humility will have both husband and wife immediately putting aside their individualized focus on themselves and beginning to acknowledge their spouse. She is your teammate, not your competition. In the same manner culture is built with a positive effect, it can also be built with a negative one as well.

HUMILITY

Humility is quite often a touchy subject for men as the word "submission" is for women. So, let's touch on it. What does it mean to be humble (as opposed to seeing humility as being under the control or manipulation of your wife)? Humility is a matter of obedience. It takes humility to obey your calling, purpose, and role in the institution of your marriage. Humility is the combination of self-awareness, servant leadership (willingness to serve), and kindness (fruits of the Spirit) toward your spouse and other people in general. Being humble is not feeling or being insignificant, inferior, subservient, or inadequate. These feelings speak to a lack of self-awareness. Self-awareness is knowing who you are, what you bring to the table, and cemented in your character and development as a man. When operating in a balanced level of self-awareness, you are not too good to do anything. Your story doesn't have to be the proverbial man who does not ask for directions. Asking for directions does not make you less of a man. Neither does acknowledging when you are wrong about something and apologizing to your wife. You are not right about anything by definition of being a part of the male gender. Most importantly, self-awareness means you also understand your purpose and role as a man in life.

Being kind to your wife is a matter of humanity. It is an expectation we should all have of one another and meet. The humility found in kindness allows for momentary disagreements, but eliminates harsh words, anger, and bitterness towards your wife. Kindness translates into respect for your wife. Humility eliminates the ego. Being a successful husband requires humility. Humility is always a great approach to get away with love.

Additionally, people tend to see their spouse as a reflection of them. With that comes an attempt to manage who they are as a tactic to reflect who you are. Your approach to the matter can be out of ego or humility. Nothing is wrong with encouraging your spouse with new approaches or ideas on life, but it is a delicate matter of love, patience, communication, and an authentic desire to help each other develop.

COLLECTIVISM VS. INDIVIDUALISM *PART 3*

I understand far too well how ambition for success can overrun a marriage when the focus moves from growth within the marriage to individual success observed by the public. My spouse at the time made it clear that she should be my first priority while her first three priorities were elsewhere. I came in around a cool fourth or fifth slot. Self-actualization for either spouse, as purposed individuals, can best be achieved with a collectivist mindset. A collectivist is someone who usually aims for answers or solutions that are beneficial for both of you and everyone else affected by a situation. An individualist is someone who primarily considers how a matter impacts them and less about others. Can you see the ego at play? Oneness is oneness; one mind, one Spirit, one team.

"How do you get away with love?" Are you dealing with some feelings of neglect by your spouse, and in this moment of time desire her full attention on a trip? In another season of your life, you may leap at the idea to visit Puerto Rico and explore the city by yourself while she's at the conference. As you see, differences don't need to come in large degrees. They are often finite in perspective, but enough to not see eye to eye and be the cause of conflict that develops, builds, and spirals out of control before you know it.

There are no right or wrong answers, only right or wrong reactions. Wrongful reactions only further support additional wrongful behavior that inevitably creates a breeding ground of contempt and animosity in the marriage. As I mentioned before, marriage is an ongoing test of character and integrity. How do you get away with love? It is important to err on the side of collectivism, a community-centered mindset. When husband and wife both procure this mentality, their aim is to consistently meet the needs of their spouse for the greater good of the marriage. This doesn't happen in a vacuum. It happens as you and your wife continue to build a culture of effective communication, a culture of forgiveness, and a culture of caring, sharing, loving, trust, honor, and respect.

The Ellison Model Principals

ON BEING FAITHFUL

Don't cheat.

EMOTIONAL MATURITY

Emotional maturity is the ability to effectively manage your attitude, behavior, and communication in times of conflict and crisis toward the end of building consensus and problem solving. Emotionally mature people are quicker to listen, take time to process information, and strategically pursue resolution as opposed to escalation. Some people are not emotionally prepared to sync their lives with someone else and make room for a whole other being to mesh into almost every decision they will make for the rest of their life as a husband or wife. Of course, many people do it. But no matter how many women give birth on a daily basis, it will never disqualify the risk she endures. Marriage is a similar risk. It's very doable, but are you prepared to do it?

The challenge in marriage, unlike our places of employment, are the economic, religious, political, psychological, and social implications that create a deep-seated emotional investment. That emotional investment creates expectations, often unstated, as to how the social contract of love and marriage should be maintained. But many aspects of the social contract were dictated to you, meaning you might be enslaved to expectations you were never in control of nor were they created by you. You are regurgitating a social curriculum that has tremendously framed your thinking. This leads to your biggest challenge, the emotional maturity to manage and resolve issues of your unmet expectations.

We are told to get married. And somewhere in the process, between the Disney movies, fairytale stories, and social contract of love and marriage, we are supposed to be prepared and almost intrinsically know what to do. It's after the divorce rate hits 50 percent we say maybe we aren't ready for what we thought we were ready for.

NURTURE YOUR MARRIAGE

Each new phase of your marriage requires a period of dedicated focus. It is like having a newborn baby. Skin-to-skin contact from its mother and father is pivotal in order to establish a connection. Similarly, you will repeatedly need a close enough relationship (skin to skin) with your wife as you both enter and exit new spaces within your marriage.

We understand best the amount of time, nurture, and focus it takes to develop a newborn baby. The parents' presence is the most valuable asset for a child. By presence I mean actively present, which, simplified is a discussion of time. What you do in that time becomes the next quintessential question. But you first have to make the time to be present.

THE EFFICACY OF BOOTY RUBS

CHAPTER 17

God is a booty God. I'm certain of it. After all, He was the chief engineer in the human design plan that included booty. I am not sure how some cultures of women seem to be without, while others seem to have an overabundance, but I'm certain if you weighed all the booty in the world it would add up to an important number that impacts the axis the world spins on. When you think about it, put two nice round booty cheeks together and you have the world in your hands. In the blessings of God, it appears as if Black and Brown women have received a double portion of booty. It is evident throughout the Caribbean and South America.

The gluteus maximus, medius, and minimus support the pelvis and hips. They are hard-working muscles that perform daily the actions of standing, walking, and supporting us when we sit. Ultimately, stress is heavily consolidated in the gluteus area. The booty rub is a holistic healing approach to combating these symptoms.

THE HISTORY

Booty rubs emanate from a painful history shared by most people. For many, our first encounter with life was with the introduction of pain when we were spanked on the booty. To cry was to be alive. Child rearing for churchgoers who upheld the mantle "spare the rod, spoil the child" meant the booties of many adolescent Christians have literally endured ass whoopings. The sliding scale of punishment ranges from a hand that pats or smacks the booty to belts, switches, sticks or whatever is in close proximity. For many, the booty has been a place of accumulated trauma.

At the same token, the booty has been a place of affection and comfort. After being welcomed to the world through a smack on the booty, it is also the place where a mother's hand tends to naturally gravitate. Newborns placed on their mother's chest for the all too important skin-to-skin contact necessary in the bonding experience of any new relationship are soothed by the gentle rub on their buttocks. This form of showing affection may easily continue for the first two years of a child's life.

THE EFFICACY

Access to touching the booty and the type of touch to the booty is a qualitative measure of the relational space between a couple. Teenage girls may allow the boy they like to run his hand across her booty. The woman in a serious dating relationship may allow him to rub her booty for an untimed duration. In a highly jovial, affectionate space, hugs may be met with double palming, in which he is free to grip and hold as much of the world as he can. In a sexual space, smacking the booty is often welcomed and encouraged.

Your relationship to her booty will inevitably become a type of expected communication within the relationship. As you walk past her in the kitchen or bedroom, as you wait in line to be seated, or at any moment the urge strikes, a gentle rub, light smack, or palming of her booty signals your presence and acknowledgement of her.

Overall, the booty rub is a mix of scientific exploration, medical practice, psychology, and mental wellness. You must master the unassuming, gentle art of the booty rub. It is a deeply programmed, non-verbal communication that places God-like powers literally in the palm of your hands. The booty rub triggers endorphins throughout the body and causes the brain to divert itself back to an infantile-like emotion. Simply put, the soothing nature of the booty rub is reminiscent of the caring emotions she felt as a newborn. That is why a booty rub during her deliberation about her work day, problem on the job, or issue with a friend effortlessly provides clarity to her emotions and receptiveness to your feedback. She is comforted through the booty rub, she is acknowledged through the booty rub, and she is aroused through the booty rub. It is a powerful practice that comes second only to a family that prays together, stays together.

The ancient art of the booty rub should not be lost on any husband dedicated to building and growing an effective relationship with their wife. The intrigue of the booty rub is found in the immediate connection it creates and the sustained healing provided for the trauma it continuously endures. As you give each other your hand in marriage, remember the relationship reflects both of your handiwork.

The booty can be viewed in three distinct but collective areas nonetheless. The lower back to the top third of her booty is the comforting zone. This area is typically rubbed during conversations while lying comfortably in a horizontal position. The middle third of her booty is the acknowledgment zone. This area is intended to be rubbed in a standing position. You may combine the top and middle portions at any time to simultaneously provide comfort and acknowledge her presence. The middle third is also appropriate for light to medium smacking. The bottom third is the arousal zone, intended for cuffing, heavy smacking, and single and double palming. The middle and bottom third may be combined to signal acknowledgement and lovemaking interest. Note that any zone may be accessible, but booty rubbing should be carefully approached with your best efforts to consider time and place and the quality of your relationship. Rub on.

GET MARRIED & MAKE IT LAST

CHAPTER 18

Marriage Is beautiful. I fully believe in the sanctity, purpose, and pleasure of marriage. Finding a person to spiritually, emotionally, and physically share this life with while reflecting God's love to each other and those in your sphere of influence is Heaven on earth. It is a state of perfection for which we are called to achieve. In turn, men and women can go through the process of life building tradition, changing history, demonstrating character, shaping personalities, promoting creativity, creating legacy, and making a legend of love. Marriage reflects the divine oneness that was intended for Adam and Eve. Accordingly, we can understand why such a strong negative force works against the success of marriages. But…

Imagine if we got it right. Imagine if we dedicated ourselves to upholding the bond of peace, preferring one another, the interest to share in a space of love, fellowship, and understanding with unconditional love. We would really experience trickle-down economics because charity begins at home. You might have heard the following comment in reference to a co-worker or supervisor when they appear to have a bad attitude: "They need to get some." Why do we say that? Because we innately understand that the starting point of our day and our lives begins with the space we share in our family, especially our significant other. We attribute the bad attitude to them needing to "get some" love, attention, or affection from their significant other.

What we are really saying is that love, attention, and affection from our significant other translates into experiencing a colleague with a better mood, which creates a better working environment, possibly a more productive work environment, wherein processes that affect the organization may be handled with more compassion, respect, honor, and trust. This in turns creates an environment with better morale. The better morale is reciprocated back at home because the negative effects of work don't spill over into our personal lives where we might otherwise take out our anger or frustration on the people closest to us. I'm not attempting to make Utopia happen. But imagine if we got it right. The love, attention, and affection communicated between husband and wife will certainly transmit to the children, who in turn grow up with those values, and as world leaders, make better choices for the sake of humanity that reflects the same love, attention, and affection back to the people they serve.

Amidst a noisy world of misinformation, the paradigm shift that realigned my perception of women, in spite of my past hurts and perception and perspectives, was the revelation that a wife and husband are gifts to each other. She's not a business partner, albeit she will gift you with business ideas. She's not the mother of your children, albeit she will most likely birth your children. She's not your confidant, albeit she should be your best friend. All of those things are secondary. She is first and foremost a gift. And everything she is capable of providing to you in the marriage is just part of the **gift that keeps on giving**. You should take care of your gift. Tend to it. Ensure its safety. Be thankful for it. Maximize its potential. Learn how to work it. Understand its parts. The benefits of your gift are benefits back to you. The awesome part is that you are a gift back to her and she should be the same for you. We can further understand marriage by understanding there are two marriages at play in every marriage. The first marriage occurs long before you ever propose to your wife.

THE FIRST MARRIAGE

The first marriage occurs within the spiritual alignment of an individual long before the external marriage to your wife. The same goes for her. Successful marriages begin at the spiritual level for both spouses. In order to understand the internal marriage of spiritual alignment, it is imperative to know that before being a husband, you must first be a wife. I know that may sound strange, but allow me to elaborate and tie together biblical precepts around this point.

Every woman and man exists as both an Earth-bound creature in a physical body and also as a spiritual being. The Bible develops a clear understanding regarding the Church as the bride of Christ. Christ, referred to as the bridegroom, died for the sins of the Church (His bride) with the expectation that each person will repent and be baptized (Acts 2:38) and come into the covenant (marriage) with Him. In effect, the male to female relationship is symbolic of the Christ to Church relationship. When the male entity recognizes his spiritual composition is part of the Church (the Body of Christ), he then takes on the posture of wife to Christ. At the level of the spirit, the term husband and wife does not reflect physical gender. Wife represents a position or role in which Christ (husband) has an expectation of you and you (wife) of him in this spiritual relationship. As wife, your submission is found in Matthew 22:37, "Thou shalt love the Lord thy God with all thy heart, and with all thy soul, and with all thy mind." The act of submission is a wifely act. Husbands, you are a spiritual wife to your Earthbound wife, as she is a spiritual wife to you as well.

Furthermore, Christ (husband) has indicated that He is your Jehovah-Jireh (provider) and Jehovah-El Elohim (protector). Psalms 46 also describes Him as our refuge and strength. In response to His husbandry, the man's wifely duty back to Christ is also found in Galatians 5:22-23, which says the fruits of the Spirit are love, joy, peace, longsuffering, gentleness, goodness, faith, meekness, and temperance. In addition to obedience, submission, humility, power and a sound mind, the role of a wife is to demonstrate these Christ qualities. Remember, in marriage you become one: one body (of Christ), one Spirit, one faith, and one baptism. Therefore, your Earthly marriage is reflective of your spiritual marriage.

At this juncture, when Christ "finds" a wife, He then finds a "good thing" in you. But you can't find yourself. He finds you (wife) and cultivates you back to Himself. That is a spiritual process. Christ's Scriptural praise of our "good" as His wife is found in Matthew 25:23 when He states, "Well done, good and faithful servant." The alternative is His rebuke found in Matthew 7:23, "I never knew you: depart from me, ye that work iniquity."

The Earth-bound woman has the same mandate for being a spiritual wife. She too is required, as part of the Church, to establish the right attitude with Christ, her first husband. You don't want a woman to submit to you as a man. You want a wife that engages you with a spiritual compass. A woman must demonstrate her spirituality to you as you do the same to her. A husband is not required to be more spiritually aligned than his wife. A woman does not have the right nor is permitted by her gender to be less godly or spiritual. A woman is equally responsible for the success of her relationship and for making spirituality the center of the marriage. She too has to first be married to Christ as a spiritual wife.

THE SECOND MARRIAGE

The second marriage occurs at the natural level with your wife. It comes with wedding bells, a honeymoon, and court documents filed with the county. However, the wife that you are to Christ will reflect in the husband you are to your wife. If you do not operate out of the fruits of the Spirit in your relationship as a spiritual wife, how effective can you be as a husband to your Earthbound wife? Again, you must first be a wife before you can be a husband. It is similar to the concept you have to follow before you can lead. Note, if the attributes of being a spiritual wife are the same as being a good husband to your natural wife, and if the attributes of being a spiritual wife are the same for her in being a good wife to you, in effect, you have Christ as the head of the marriage and the man and woman operating as wives toward each other. Perfecto. Christ is the true head of the household on which both natural husband and wife should remain spiritually focused. No different from Jehovah as protector and provider, if the fruits of the Spirit are what they are, then our best position as a husband is being a wife.

COSMOPOLITAN LEADERSHIP VIA THE ELLISON MODEL

The leadership style traditionally expressed by the Bible centers on servant-leadership. Unfortunately, the residue of the individualistic mentality of Westernized countries permeates our understanding of servant leadership, further skewing how we perceive the institution of marriage. Servant leadership is a fading altruism because people tend to want a servant leader for their individualistic-minded needs. Servant leadership then becomes an opportunity for the person receiving the service to look out for themselves first, including their goals, their dreams, their desires, their worth, and their gains. We have to go beyond servant leadership in order to make relationships work.

I believe women need a different style of leader in their life. In a world that now produces many more progressive, college educated, and entrepreneurially-minded women, an enhanced style of leadership that embraces their potential is of the utmost importance. Cosmopolitan leadership is an ideal start.

In the book *Contemporary Conflict Resolution* by Oliver Ramsbotham, Tom Woodhouse, and Hugh Hall, cosmopolitan places a focus on "**recognizing the richness of the resources across cultures and religions**." Ramsbotham et al. also cites Ulrich Beck's definition of cosmopolitan found in *The Cosmopolitan Vision*, which is to acknowledge 'otherness,' including "**the otherness of those who are culturally different, the otherness of the future, the otherness of nature, the otherness of the object, and the otherness of rationalities.**" Women in the 21ST century represent the epitome of this "otherness." The 21ST century is the Age of Women, a time and place in which their leadership, rationalities, and execution will inevitably and have already begun to be actualized.

The most important work in transforming marriages and the overall relationship between men and women begins with the ways in which men (and women) perceive women. Men and women must reimagine and re-envision women. Many men adopt traditional values that inherently subjugate women into a very limited occupation of life. Men must acknowledge women and their vast capacity to be effective leaders.

Simultaneously, women must also reimagine and re-envision themselves out of the box in which patriarchal societies have placed them while also recognizing the ways that society has subjugated men with social norms that are just as overwhelming and overbearing. It's a civil war on love and marriage—a fight for recognition, acknowledgement, validation, and vindication of social norms that we are victims to and not the authors of.

Women must demand their rightful, justified existence. However, women cannot go to the other extreme. In that case, they become the matriarchs of power and hyperfemininity, dominating men in similar ways in which men have dominated women. Throughout this book, I have constructed an intricate argument to highlight the ways in which women have the capacity and often take the liberty to victimize men and game the system by appropriating masculinity. No one is the better for it. But we are all the better for understanding the equality amongst men and women and the right to share and participate in the access and resources of our emerging world.

I implore you to see her beyond the dominant dialogue that has informed your thinking from birth. See her for the capacity to bring life into this world and a suitable partner with whom to build your legacy. Hold yourself accountable. Also, hold her accountable for your and her own sake. And most of all, be compassionate as you both work to reimagine and re-envision man and woman, husband and wife, and the many other roles we play in our lives.

Cosmopolitan leaders understand the strength of inclusion across a globalized world, demonstrate multicultural appreciation, embrace reciprocal mentorship across those cultural lines, resolve conflict through a global thought process, and build sustainable relationships with a broad understanding of the global market. Women fall into this category of globalization as they too have expanded into active social, economic, and political contributors to our international society. As women have been provided access to higher education, broader experiences in the workplace, and opportunities for upward mobility on their own merit, landing them at the table of influencers and decision makers, their input has proven to be just as valuable as any other man. Contrary to some biblical interpretations, women are no longer second-class citizens designed to be homemakers. Women sit as prime ministers, CEOs, presidents, and other high-level officials. They are highly educated, entrepreneurial, innovative, creative, and driven individuals who have finally been given a rightful platform to co-exist alongside men. This type of inclusion is adaptation, growth, and inclusion of new technology as the world around us evolves. Women are part of that evolution. A cosmopolitan leader embraces these attributes. Note, King Lemuel's mother described this cosmopolitan woman in the Book of Proverbs 31, written in 700 BC.

While much of the women's movement has come with some emasculation of men, I acknowledge that women have pressed forward through hurt and heartbreak from a systematic design that has historically not made room for her input. As it relates to marriage, cosmopolitan leadership understands the dynamism of your wife and embraces and plans for it in your approach to married life. Cosmopolitan leadership is a broad approach that does not relegate her to just one 'territory' of life, but allows her a passport to share in the globalization of leadership, innovation, and direction of the marriage. In other words, neither of you are bordered by definition of your gender. Your wife might very well be the next President of the United States of America.

Many of our Christian religious cues about marriage are prescribed to servant-leadership. The story of Jesus propels the understanding of selflessness and service to others, a trait that is viewed as necessary for marriage. Women no longer need 'service' in the traditional ways we have been groomed to think, nor does she 'serve' in the same capacity we have been traditionally taught to expect. It's inappropriate to expect the service of dinner, prepared by your wife, as a mandate after she has worked her 40-hour job. She now shares an expanded role far removed from the 1950s. Servant-leadership, the leadership style largely expressed by the Bible, is not lost in cosmopolitan leadership, it is subsumed.

THE WE CONVERSATION VIA THE ELLISON MODEL

The effectiveness of cosmopolitan leadership is affirmed in the We Conversation, an inclusive, communal approach that transcends traditional social norms. As the woman has become global, our attitude, behavior, and communication, along with a disciplined approach, must also enhance toward marriage. The *We Conversation* removes the centerfolding attitude demonstrated by either spouse to an overemphasis on *the We* as one body, one mind, and one spirit. As they said in the movie Drumline, "One band, one sound." We are able to more inclusively take the position that we provide for each other, we protect each other, we take care of each other, we love each other, we support each other, and we uplift each other. We can put idioms of exclusion, manipulation, and power struggles to the side such as, "If you give her a house, she will give you a home; happy wife, happy life; the man is the head, the woman is the neck; women really wear the pants; and the two of you argue like a married couple," to name a few.

After the wedding bells have ceased ringing and the honeymoon is over, what is there to sustain the relationship beyond the glitz and glamour of romance and fairytale? *The We* Conversation is an approach of sustainability. Being the breadwinner, becoming a millionaire, or any expectation toward an upper-class lifestyle is not the answer. Rich people divorce too. The *We Conversation* is a cosmopolitan leadership approach with 1) an optimistic, forward-thinking, open-minded, respectful and positive attitude, 2) a wholesome, courteous, faithful, and transparent behavior, 3) a culture of effective communication that aims to understand before seeking to be understood, and 4) being disciplined in maintaining these appropriate attitudes, behaviors, and communication. *The We* takes full effect as both partners re-socialize their perspective of what male and female interaction ought to be.

WHEN TWO CULTURES MEET

Two cultures always meet when a male and female come together in matrimony. Marriage is a cultural exchange regardless if both parties share the same ethnicity, come from the same local city, have similar educational backgrounds, and share the same spiritual beliefs. The couple still has to learn the habits, idioms, and distinct behaviors of one another.

Learning for the first time and/or having to contend with the habits, idioms, and distinct behaviors of your partner is where the work of the little fox seeks to begin its attempt to destroy the marital vine. The nucleus of the challenge stems from our personal and private behavior that has developed over the bulk of our lives while single. You have taken care of yourself for the majority of your life, in terms of tending to your daily preparation, relaxation, and dress code, among other things. And while doing so, you have developed certain personal and private behaviors that little attention is paid to, such as:

- Bedroom etiquette (sleeping formation; eating in bed; snoring)
- Toilet seat up or down
- Water running while brushing teeth
- Wet sink after washing face or brushing teeth
- Wet bathroom floor after shower
- Inability to locate keys
- Feet on furniture
- Throwing clothes down anywhere versus hanging them up
- Alcohol or smoking
- Timeliness

Personal and private behaviors that when exposed to our mate may be new, different, found to be irritating, or ultimately subject to "getting under our skin." The exposure to one's personal and private behavior can be considered a matter of cultural shock that requires overcoming. Many couples date for several years and become engaged for an additional length of time without 1) ever noticing the behaviors or its extent, or 2) being uware of the affect the behaviors will have on them when confined to that person in a small space for a long period of time. Couples must be aware that everyone has their reinforced personal and private behavior. It requires prayer and positive communication with your partner to overcome these little foxes.

WHICH WAY DO WE GO?

Like any other business, a marriage should have a purpose, a mission and a vision. A marriage should stand for something, containing solid reasons for persisting (beyond having children). Marriages should be centered on a Strategic Plan that:

- Establishes the purpose of the marriage.
- Articulates a shared vision and mission statement for the marriage.
- Sets meaningful goals and objectives for the success of the marriage.
- Creates a timeline for goal accomplishment.
- Allows for reflection and evaluation (with third-party assistance; supervisors and employees evaluate each other to learn how they can do their jobs better so that they may keep their jobs – married couples need do the same so that they may keep their marriage).

The marriage's strategic plan serves as a guide of principles, morals, and concrete objectives, highlighting and utilizing the combined skill set of the couple. It also assists in allowing each person to maintain his or her individual identity in the marriage while creating a marital identity.

MARITAL IDENTITY

A major undertaking by any business organization is defining who they are and what they stand for. With answers to that identity question, they design their products, services, and support systems to match. As mentioned before, marriage is not a business; however, it has necessary business components to the relationship to ensure proper management of its resources. Likewise, in marriage you have to work together in designing and branding your marriage according to the purpose of your relationship. And who takes out the garbage (task) has little to do with understanding your role.

The design of your marriage, which includes the management of your household, will look different from home to home. There is no one design for everyone. People have different goals, aspirations, visions, and principles that guide their spiritual, emotional, and physical beings. A husband and wife may choose to have separate bank accounts, while another couple may choose to have joint accounts. There is no right or wrong answer. Understanding your role as leaders, knowing God is your Jehovah-Jireh and Jehovah-El Elohim, and submitting yourself to the process leaves you free to make joint decisions for the prosperity of your household according to the purpose of your marriage. There is value in each person, qualities that make each person unique, special, and evoke a certain energy. That energy combined with their partner's represents the fullness of God throughout the spiritual journey. The strategic plan for one's marriage can only be established through prayer, meditation, and positive communication. Divine intervention is the only medium that is able to communicate and guide your marriage's strategic plan.

HOW TO TREAT A WOMAN

a poem

Treat her like a sheet of paper
The Pen Is mightier than the sword
The lines of her heart are properly spaced apart
To let your prayers pour
Treat her like a sheet of paper
On which privileged to write
Let pen strokes of love
Be the man you script in her life
Know her stock and weight
Be a best friend and paper-mate
Be her folder and hold her
Know how to relate
With a calligraphy of empathy
That understands her history
She needs white out to blot out
But to create the perfect picture
Sometimes you crop out
But never cop out
For inkwells of love will never dry
And paper planes don't always fly
But try
She is a novel idea
A thickening plot
A climaxing mystery
That makes you wonder who shot J.R.
But they are fiction
Write a story so deep readers think it's encryption
Subscribe as her scribe

And let your subscription to God's vision add pages to her mission
So she strolls with a confidence
Of scrolls in her providence
Treat her like a sheet of paper
That when your eyes lock, they dot
Be a pupil and a teacher
A mentee and mentor in order to reach her
Pin back her hair and scotch tape the tear
Card stock may be a challenge
But we are all under construction paper
To be constructed greater
To write what's right, like
Write day where there's night
Write peace where there's fight
Write faith where there's plight
Write truth where there's hype
Write forgiveness where there's spite
Write unity where there's strife
Write newness where there's trite
Write understanding where there's gripe
And don't take any of this light
The editor-in-chief is Christ
But you are second in command on her writing staff
Don't have the last words but let your words last
Words of love don't return void
They return receipts of certified mail
To confirm the manifestation of how love prevails
A printed copy of the principles you copy
So treat her like a sheet of paper
On which privileged to write
Let pen strokes of love
Be the man you script in her life.

ABOUT THE AUTHOR

Adrian N. Carter, PhDc is a doctoral candidate in the Conflict Resolution Studies program at Nova Southeastern University in Davie, FL. His research focus is on the identity, emotion, and power of men, specifically examining race relations, gender roles, and the education system and how they create interpersonal and organizational conflict amongst men and society.

Adrian is a sought-after keynote speaker, conflict resolution practitioner, and leadership development trainer who has been impacting corporations and educational institutions for 20 years with his dynamic and progressive ability to lead and help others build solutions. Adrian's conflict resolution practice includes conflict coaching, executive coaching, facilitative dialogue, mediation, leadership development, and conflict resolution training for corporate and educational entities, and consulting for small business development.

Founder of the EmpowerMEN Conference, a male empowerment initiative focused on conflict resolution training, leadership development, and redefining the identity of men in the 21ST century, Adrian teaches interpersonal and organizational leadership using the multi-faceted leadership development tool, The Ellison Model. The seven major content areas of The Ellison Model make it an effective and solution-oriented tool for corporate and educational institutions. The Ellison Model was developed by world-class sociologist, professor, and mentor Dr. Deryl G. Hunt. Adrian firmly upholds his mentor's mantra, "It's not the problem that counts—it's the solution."

Ultimately, Adrian is a social scientist and thought leader committed to influencing people through his training, publications, and poetry into becoming more caring, sharing, and loving individuals. Adrian is a father of three. When he is not speaking, teaching, and training, Adrian enjoys writing and performing spoken word poetry, doing music production, and graphic design. To date, Adrian has published three books of poetry titled *Lovebook I*, *Lovebook II*, and *Song of Adrian: Lovebook III*. Adrian N. Carter is your solution expert, calibrated for leadership in the 21ST century with integrity and a deep care for teaching, learning, and approaching the social world with renewed ideas for inclusive community building.

ALSO BY ADRIAN N. CARTER

Emerging as the Right Person in the Right Place at the Right Time: Leadership in the 21ST Century Using The Ellison Model

Song of Adrian: Lovebook III

Lovebook II: Perfectly joined together

Lovebook I: Unto the measure of the stature of the fulness of poetry

Lovebear's Heartstrings
(Spoken Word Album)

Perfectly Joined Together
(Spoken Word Album)

ACKNOWLEDGMENTS

Dad, thank you for growing through this process with me. I know watching your son and grandchildren go through this transition was a testing situation for you as well. But you showed kindness and a willingness to understand matters in ways you had not before. Mom (Joann), thank you as well for bearing with me through it all. You were encouraging and giving in my time of need. I love and appreciate you in so many ways. I will always feel remorseful for being a difficult child. But you loved me anyways. Mom (Sonia), thank you for always wanting the best for your son.

Laura A., you did not have to continue believing in me, but you did, even when others did not. You were a beacon of encouragement during this dark transition to light. I did not know meeting you in the master's program would have led us to such an amazing and empowering friendship, but I am grateful. Tell Joe I said hello.

Jennifer F., I think we have solved all the world's problems in our conversations. I wish our phone calls were recorded. Thank you for having a balancing perspective and being a sounding board of reason, compassion, and insight. We have more work to do.

Clive, Duncan, Just John, and J. Horne, Lawrence, thank you for being my brothers in arms that propped me up on so many occasions.

Marianne and Alicia, you two are my sisters for real. I love what we have grown to in love, understanding, and loyalty. Everybody wins when the family fuels. Thank you for being a part of my purpose and family jewels.

Crystal (my Godsister), thank you for texting and calling just to say, "Adrian, I love you." It meant so, so much. I often felt alone, exiled to an island by myself. But your "I love yous" were planks that helped me build a raft back to a peace of mind.

Eccentrich and Elaina, the hours on the phone were countless, but you listened. Thank you for taking the time to understand the other side to a story that appears to be often overlooked.

To my doctoral colleagues and friends at Nova Southeastern University, Radar and Peren, thank you for being a part of my process. The conflict resolution studies program built new friendships and commitments that I hope will be productive and last a lifetime.

Unequally yoked?

CPSIA information can be obtained
at www.ICGtesting.com
Printed in the USA
BVHW031200190720
583828BV00006B/142

9 781953 156006